Contents

THE BRIDGE

Complete Poems of Hart Crane

Edited by Marc Simon

Liveright

New York • London

ISBN 0-87140-656-X
ISBN 0-87140-178-9 pbk.

Liveright Publishing Corporation, 500 Fifth Avenue, New York, N.Y. 10110
www.wwnorton.com

W. W. Norton & Company Ltd.
Castle House, 75/76 Wells St., London, W1T 3QT

3 4 5 6 7 8 9 0

KEY WEST   *An Island Sheaf*

KEY WEST   Folder Subsection

Poems Uncollected but Published by Crane

Poems Unpublished by Crane

Incomplete Works

Fragments

Centenary Introduction
by Harold Bloom

He has reason, as all the philosophic and poetic class have: but he has also, what they have not,—this strong solving sense to reconcile his poetry with the appearances of the world, and build a bridge from the streets of cities to the Atlantis.

—EMERSON ON PLATO

I

Born in 1930, the year Hart Crane published *The Bridge*, I never reflect on that year of my birth without also meditating upon Crane's visionary epic. I begin in this fashion, because my early (and continued) love for Hart Crane's poetry was typical of many other critics and of many poets in my generation. I began reading Hart Crane in 1940, incessantly renewing the *Collected Poems* from the Melrose branch of the Bronx Public Library, returning the volume only when my sister gave me the book for my twelfth birthday. It was the first book I ever owned, and is with me still. Crane's poetry has been a touchstone for me, and remains central to a fully imaginative understanding of American literature. His American precursors were Emerson, Whitman, Emily Dickinson, Wallace Stevens, and (in style, rather than vision) T. S. Eliot. If you add Hart Crane himself to that sequence, then you would have (with the addition of Robert Frost) the major American poets, in my judgment.

I write this Introduction in August/October 1999, a century after Harold Hart Crane was born in Garrettsville, Ohio, on July 21, 1899. Crane died at sea, apparently a suicide, on April 27, 1932, three months before what would have been his thirty-third birthday. One thinks of Shelley, drowned at twenty-nine (evidently by accident), and of Keats, consumed by tuberculosis before he was twenty-six. Crane's poetic gifts were of their order of magnitude, and surpassed those even of Whitman, Dickinson, Eliot, Frost, Stevens. All of them, dead at thirty-two, would have had a truncated achievement. The work of Hart Crane's poetic maturity, on the basis of "The Broken Tower" and some final fragments, could have surpassed in eminence anything else in our national tradition.

Crane is a difficult poet, intensely metaphorical and allusive. Combined with his transcendental yearnings, and his high invocatory style, his logic of metaphor characteristically gives us the sensation of an impacted density, sometimes resistant to unraveling. His "rhetoricity" or verbal self-consciousness can be extraordinary, and suggests affinities with Christopher Marlowe and Gerard Manley Hopkins as well as with T. S. Eliot. Despite Crane's Dionysiac personality and Orphic doom-eagerness, he was an obsessive revisionist of his own work, as his manuscripts demonstrate. A Pindaric celebrant, Crane was as deliberate an artist as American poetry affords. This can give the effect of paradox; *The Bridge,* though very varied, is frequently a dithyramb, carrying the reader along on a cascade of ecstatic sound. Ecstasy, by no means always erotic, is prevalent in Crane's poetry. He is a rhapsode, like the Shelley of *Prometheus Unbound.* If you read Emerson's essay on "The Poet," which inspired Whitman, you are likelier to think of Crane than of Whitman. The Orphic poet of America, eloquently prophesied by Emerson, turned out to be Hart Crane.

And yet Crane was an anomaly in his generation, surrounded by poet-critics like Yvor Winters, Allen Tate, Richard P. Blackmur, and Malcolm Cowley. Having discussed Crane with all of them, I always found myself saddened by their affectionate misunderstanding of his achievement. His deepest affinities in his generation were with Kenneth Burke, who remarked to me that he came to a fully sympathetic perception of Crane's work largely after the poet's death. The Age of Eliot and Pound was not a benign context for Crane, a High Romantic in the era of High Modernism and the Eliotic New Criticism, committed to judging any Romantic's sensibility as "dissociated." Crane, divided in several psychic regards, nevertheless had a dangerously unified sensibility, by Eliot's test, which is to fuse together thought, emotion, sensation, actually Walter Pater's critical vision before it became Eliot's.

2

Crane, not yet seventeen, already wrote in his characteristic modes; clearly he unfolded almost as much as he developed. Genius is a mystery resistant to reductive analysis, whether sociobiological, psychological, or historical. Like Milton, Pope, and Tennyson, the youthful Crane was a consecrated poet before he was an adolescent. An era like that of the last third of the twentieth century hardly knows what to make of a poet like Hart Crane, who had no political interests whatsoever. Crane's temperament resembled Shelley's; the invocatory drive of *Adonais* is echoed in "Atlantis," the conclusion of *The Bridge* but the first section to be composed. Yet Shelley's politics were pragmatic as well as Platonic. Crane had a more personal project, in renewal of Whitman's: to fuse the myth of America with a realized homoeroticism. So overt and harrowing is Crane's erotic quest that attempts to analyze it from the stance of a "homosexual poetic" seem to me quite redundant, and bound to fail. Critics of that persuasion repeat ineptly what Crane conveys with mordant skill.

A professed Nietzschean, Crane renews the Pindaric vision of the *agon*, in which the poetic spirit must unfold itself in fighting. Fascinated by Wallace Stevens's artistry, Crane had no quarrel with the equally Romantic Stevens. Eliot's *The Waste Land*, from the moment of its appearance, was Crane's inevitable antagonist. In Crane's struggle against Eliot, there are ironies of which Crane may not have been aware. Crane is the overt Whitmanian, and yet *The Bridge* does not have so close a relationship to any major poem by Whitman, even "Crossing Brooklyn Ferry," as *The Waste Land* does to "When Lilacs Last in the Dooryard Bloom'd," Eliot's hidden paradigm. Eliot takes from Whitman the lilacs, the hermit thrush, the murmur of maternal lamentation, the self-surrender of giving up the tally or sexual existence, and even the vision of three walking together down the road to an equivocal salvation.

Walt Whitman, subtlest and most hermetic of American poets, actually is more of a real (if covert) presence in T. S. Eliot and Wallace Stevens, than he is in Hart Crane. Though Crane sought to affirm Whitman against Eliot, the elegiac, negative Whitman, his Real Me or Me Myself, pervades Eliot and Stevens. Crane's more Emersonian Whitman is dangerous to summon up, as the "Cape Hatteras" section of *The Bridge* demonstrates. And Crane's "logic of metaphor," his associative rhetoric, is not at all Whitmanian. Shadowed by Eliot's style, Crane wins autonomy by returning to Emily Dickinson as prime American ancestor, and to Christopher Marlowe and William Blake as English precursors. Stevens's *Harmonium* aided the young Crane in holding off Eliot, but then Stevens suffered poetic silence until *Ideas of Order*, published after Crane's early death.

The Waste Land (1922), which never departed from Allen Tate's verse, and which blocked Robert Penn Warren from a voice of his own until *Incarnations* (1968), had its most ambivalent effect upon all of Hart Crane's work from 1922 to 1932, when Crane's life and career destroyed one another. Canonization, now so absurdly derided, is not the work either of academic-journalistic sects, or even of the few strong critics, like Kenneth Burke and William Empson. The irony of canonization is that it is always the labor of strong poets, novelists, story-writers, dramatists who come after, belated but still agonistic. As a Stevensian, I happily endorse his strictures upon the poems of X (Eliot), which is that "they do not make the visible / a little hard to see." But after a lifetime of disliking Eliot's literary and "cultural" criticism, I have to yield to *The Waste Land,* because Hart Crane did, though he went down fighting the poem. The glory of *The Bridge* (1930) is its ambivalent warfare with *The Waste Land,* without which Crane would not have been the miracle he was. I say this most reluctantly, having loved Hart Crane, Blake, and Shelley since I was a child, and having loathed Eliot endlessly, even as I involuntarily memorized every line of his poetry. I take it that my ambivalence toward *The Waste Land* is essentially an inheritance from Crane, a recognition I derive from Kenneth Burke, who mentored me from about 1973 on, and who was (with Walker Evans and Malcolm Cowley) one of my links to Crane, since I was two years old when my favorite poet perished. Burke, always genial and shrewd, taught me to ask: What is the poet (or critic) trying to do for herself, *as a person,* by writing her poem or essay? Swerving from the magnificent Burke, I tend to rephrase that as: What is the poet (or critic) trying to do for herself *as a poet or critic* by composing her poem or essay? What Crane, in his seven-year agon (1923–1930) to compose *The Bridge,* sought to do for himself as poet was not less than everything, and so survival as a person was intimately involved. Empson once told me that he had a late conversion to Crane because only Crane showed how much poetry had become "a mug's game," a desperate struggle to stay alive. I read this as

Crane's gamble upon *The Bridge* (and finally upon "The Broken Tower")—if *they* demonstrated that he still had the shaping spirit in him, then he would stay alive. If not, not.

Crane, who suffered forever the curse of sundered parentage, never could settle upon a single erotic partner, hence his quest for every sailor in his generation. But I doubt—after reading Paul Mariani, the best of Crane's biographers—that a happy domestic life, and even a steady income, would have saved Crane. No nature could have been less compromising; like a new Byron or Shelley, Crane was a Pilgrim of the Absolute. His quest was for agonistic supremacy, against Eliot, in order to join Whitman, Dickinson, Melville in the American Pantheon. No one can read all of Crane's poetry, across sixty years as I have, and miss the accents of the Sublime, of the Nietzschean quest for the foremost place. Since Crane is, in his unchurched way, a great religious poet, a Shelleyan myth-maker hymning an Alien God, the tonalities of transcendence haunt *The Bridge* and "The Broken Tower," and even the erotic raptures and anguishes of "For the Marriage of Faustus and Helen" and the "Voyages." Crane, who met Lorca once, is more in the mode of Luis Cernuda, whose poetry I suspect he did not know. Farther back are Crane's deepest Hispanic affinities, with Luis de Leon, and with Juan de la Cruz, whose "Obscure Night of the Soul" finds its brother in Crane's superb invocation, "Proem: To Brooklyn Bridge."

3

It is misleading to read *White Buildings* (1926) and *The Bridge* in sequence, since most of *The Bridge* was composed 1923–1927, and "Repose of Rivers," one of Crane's best lyrics, dates from 1926. Someday there will be a Variorum Crane, that prints all of his work in chronological order of composition. *The Bridge*, in particular, would be clarified if it opened with "Atlantis," the final section of his design, yet the ecstatic inception of the visionary epic. Alas, the three weakest parts of *The Bridge*—"Cape Hatteras," "Indiana," "Quaker Hill"—were the last to be finished by a poet in despair, conscious that he had damaged his gift.

There is then no authentic distinction to be made between the lyric and the epic Crane, except that *The Bridge* does not reduce to the brilliance and coherence of its best sections. Something of Crane's vision survives the formal inadequacy of the poem's continuities. *The Waste Land*, Crane's anti-model, is aided by its curiously Whitmanian: "These fragments I have shored against my ruins," a line that would fit well enough in Whitman's *Sea-Drift* elegy, "As I Ebb'd with the Ocean of Life." But *The Bridge* needs to be more than fragments, and it is.

Still, it is a puzzle that the best poems in *The Bridge* are so complete in themselves: "Proem: To Brooklyn Bridge," "The River," "The Dance," "The Tunnel," "Atlantis." The poems of middle merit—"Ave Maria," "The Harbor Dawn," "Van Winkle," "Cutty Sark"—gain most by their context, while the "Three Songs" remain an enigma. Whether *The Bridge* gives as much to "Indiana," "Cape Hatteras," and "Quaker Hill," as they subtract from it, is disputable. Perhaps it is wisest, for now, to regard *The Bridge* as a suite or poetic sequence of fifteen poems (taking the "songs" separately). You need to know Crane's letters and his life very well in order to recapture the daemonic force that unified *The Bridge* in its poet's aspiring consciousness. The myth presented in *The Bridge* was also the myth that Hart Crane lived, at excruciating cost. His letters, which seem to me as revelatory and valuable as those of John Keats, are best read in *O My Land, My Friends*, edited by Langdon Hammer and Brom Weber. Crane's life is most vividly rendered by Paul Mariani in *The Broken Tower*. If you flank *Complete Poems of Hart Crane* by his letters and his life, then you may be surprised to see *The Bridge* fuse together for you.

Unity, whether in a long poem or short, is largely a function of the reader's perspective. Whatever their individual (and differing) dreams of poetic unity, both T. S. Eliot and Hart Crane wrote disjunctive major poems or sequences. For an Eliotic critic, like Allen Tate, cultural ideologies shared with Eliot imposed unities of which I remain skeptical, but then I am a Cranean or High Romantic critic. What allied Eliot and Crane (despite Crane's desires) were their common ambitions for making the lyric mode perform the work of the epic. David Bromwich sensitively argues that both poets were somewhat misled by these "encyclopedic ambitions." I am wary of such an argument; surely it would also apply to Wallace Stevens's long meditative sequences, that seem to me the principal glory of American poetry since *Song of Myself*. Eliot's authentic precursors were Tennyson and Whitman: *In Memoriam* and *Maud* also are curiously encyclopedic poems. The transformation of lyric into epic was a Romantic *praxis* long before it was Modernist. Coleridge's *The Rime of the Ancient Mariner* has the form of an extended ballad, and yet its scope is nearly as apocalyptic as Blake's "brief epics" or the marvelous fragments, Shelley's *The Triumph of Life* and Keats's *The Fall of Hyperion*.

Eliot and Crane (though Eliot tended to deny this poetic heritage until near his death) shared Romantic tradition and Walt Whitman. That, and the contaminating power of Eliot's verse, is why Crane's contest with Eliot was so poignant, and Crane's pragmatic victory so heroic. You can trace many allusions to Eliot in Crane, but the two styles remain powerfully antithetical:

O Lord Thou pluckest me out
O Lord Thou pluckest

burning

That is Eliot, fusing the Buddha's Fire Sermon and St. Augustine's sense of salvation. Crane, a religious myth-maker but not a believer in any orthodoxy, achieves a greater eloquence, agonistically set against Eliot:

> Kiss of our agony Thou gatherest,
>   O Hand of Fire
>   gatherest—

Who or what is such a "Thou" in *The Bridge*? Hart Crane's kind of negative transcendence represents what ought to be called the American Religion, a gnosis endemic in the United States where, for at least two centuries now, religion has been not the opiate, but the poetry of the people. Crane's actual religious heritage was his mother's Christian Science, which never affected him. In the spiritual exaltation of "The Proem: To Brooklyn Bridge," as in the spiritual anguish of "The Broken Tower," one can hear a mystical yearning that renders Hart Crane akin to St. John of the Cross, in sensibility though not in faith. Crane's deep attachment to William Blake's poetry, and to Emily Dickinson's, reflects his own stance as an autonomous visionary, distrustful of every creed or ideology, yet questing always for intimations of transcendence.

Emerson is the American fountainhead of such intimations, but it is never easy to identify Emerson's "God in me," the principle of Self-reliance. The Sage of Concord was equally adroit at evading religion and philosophy. There is an Orphic Emerson, ancestor of the Orphic Crane, but you don't locate him by searching most of his pages. Crane, at his most rhapsodic, hymns a nameless Everpresence, a kind of American version of the Gnostic Alien or Stranger God, but Emerson resolutely harbors a deity wholly within. The visionary of *The Bridge* needed more than that, but never found what he needed.

4

In April 1924, three months short of his twenty-fifth birthday, Crane began to write his "Kubla Khan" or absolute lyric, "Voyages II":

> —And yet this great wink of eternity,
> Of rimless floods, unfettered leewardings,
> Samite sheeted and processioned where
> Her undinal vast belly moonward bends,
> Laughing the wrapt inflections of our love;
>
> Take this Sea, whose diapason knells
> On scrolls of silver snowy sentences,
> The sceptred terror of whose sessions rends
> As her demeanors motion well or ill,
> All but the pieties of lovers' hands.
>
> And onward, as bells off San Salvador
> Salute the crocus lustres of the stars,
> In these poinsettia meadows of her tides,—
> Adagios of islands, O my Prodigal,
> Complete the dark confessions her veins spell.
>
> Mark how her turning shoulders wind the hours,
> And hasten while her penniless rich palms
> Pass superscription of bent foam and wave,—
> Hasten, while they are true,—sleep, death, desire,
> Close round one instant in one floating flower.
>
> Bind us in time, O Seasons clear, and awe.
> O minstrel galleons of Carib fire,
> Bequeath us to no earthly shore until
> Is answered in the vortex of our grave
> The seal's wide spindrift gaze toward paradise.

In Walt Whitman, there is a visionary fusion of four figures: night, death, the mother, and the sea. The composite metaphor for the fusion is erotic merging, largely implicit in Whitman, wholly explicit in Crane. It is useful to observe that Hart Crane was a superb reader of poetry, superior in my judgment to all the critics of his generation, except for Kenneth Burke. Crane's best insights into his precursors, marvelous though his letters are, come in Crane's own poems. I had read Whitman for years, puzzled by his recurrent use of the word "tally," but did not see what Whitman was doing with "tally" until I had brooded sufficiently upon a passage of "Cape Hatteras" in *The Bridge:*

> O, upward from the dead
> Thou bringest tally, and a pact, new bound
> Of living brotherhood!

The "tally" is the mark of the covenant between Crane and Whitman, a brotherhood certainly homoerotic, yet Crane was too good a reader not to recognize how auto-erotic Whitman's tallies tend to be. "Tally" is Whitman's most crucial metaphor, playing upon the idea of a double or an agreement. The word goes back to the Latin *talea,* a twig or cutting, like the sprig of lilac that Whitman throws upon Lincoln's coffin in the great elegy, "When Lilacs Last in the Dooryard Bloom'd." The *talea* is a stick upon which count is kept, as in Crane's "The Broken Tower": "my long-scattered score / Of broken intervals," where Crane refers both to the cognitive music of his poems and the desperate trajectory of his sexual affairs—"But not for long to hold each desperate choice." Walt Whitman brings upward from the dead a new covenant of tally: "My knowledge my live parts, it keeping tally with the meaning of all things" (*Song of Myself,* 25).

With Whitman ("Chanting the Square Deific"), Crane at his anguished close could have said: "All sorrow, labor, suffering, I, tallying it, absorb in myself." "Tally," as Crane superbly understood, is Whitman's metaphor for the covenant that binds together the poet's uneasily fused identities: erotic, creative, prophetic, the "foreshadowing and foreshortening" vision of origins that John T. Irwin superbly traces in *The Bridge*. Irwin, whose still-ongoing study of Crane's poetry is likely to be close to definitive, finds in Crane's Whitman "the image of Faustian flight." Like his precursor, Christopher Marlowe, Crane could have known that the first Faustian flight was the death-leap of Simon Magus, the Gnostic who took the cognomen, Faustus or "the favored one," when he voyaged to Rome, there to compete with the early Christians, who asserted that he died when he attempted levitation. Crane's own leap to a Caribbean death is prefigured in "Voyages II" where the Sea, an undine or mermaid-temptress, is at one with Whitman's "fierce old mother [who] endlessly cries for her castaways" ("As I Ebb'd with the Ocean of Life"). "Voyages I" had ended with the admonition: "The bottom of the sea is cruel." That inspires the: "—And yet" that begins "Voyages II," a qualification that by no means repeals the Sea's cruelty. Crane's lyrical masterpiece is celebratory of erotic completion, but like Coleridge's "Kubla Kahn" it, too, is a gorgeous procession that concludes with a visionary defeat. The style of "Voyages II" is so elliptical (more even than Crane's usual *praxis*) that the sixteen verbs employed in its twenty-five lines almost all seem quite negative in regard to the lovers' passion that supposedly is being hailed. Where the sea's "undinal vast belly moonward bends," are not homoerotic male lovers mocked? The ellipsis in the next line then would be: "Laughing [at] the wrapt inflections of our love." There is a menace in many of the verbs that follow: "knells," "rends," "pass superscription," "close round," and the equivocal "bind us in time," with its hint of Crane's covenant with Whitman, the shared tally. All the "Voyages" journey to a covenant that yields up the tally in return for "the imaged Word," which necessarily trades erotic loss for poetic gain, as here in the conclusion to "Voyages VI":

> Creation's blithe and petalled word
> To the lounged goddess when she rose
> Conceding dialogue with eyes
> That smile unsearchable repose—
>
> Still fervid covenant, Belle Isle,
> —Unfolded floating dais before
> Which rainbows twine continual hair—
> Belle Isle, white echo of the oar!
>
> The imaged Word, it is, that holds
> Hushed willows anchored in its glow.
> It is the unbetrayable reply
> Whose accent no farewell can know.

Crane revises here his own "Belle Isle," a discarded lyric written early in 1923. The "Voyages" are a Caribbean sequence, but Belle Isle is a strait between Labrador and Newfoundland, an entrance to the Gulf of St. Lawrence. There is a fine lyric, "North Labrador," in *White Buildings*, whose theme is lovelessness, but "Belle Isle" is a poem of lost love, and of its "after-word" that is transmuted into "the imaged Word" of "Voyages VI." What moved Crane to return to "Belle Isle" at the close of the ecstatic "Voyages," a homage to the relationship he had shared with the sailor Emil Opffer, the love of his life (but not of Opffer's)?

The "lounged goddess" and "unfolded floating dais" refer to Botticelli's "Birth of Venus," probably in Walter Pater's powerful evocation in *The Renaissance:*

> Men go forth to their labours until the evening; but she is awake before them, and you might think that the sorrow in her face was at the thought of the whole long day of love yet to come.... What is unmistakable is the sadness with which he

has conceived the goddess of pleasure, as the depositary of a great power over the lives of men.

We can surmise that the governing deity of the "Voyages" fuses Pater's sadomasochistic Venus and Whitman's fierce old mother, a fusion that displaces Grace Hart Crane, the poet's endlessly difficult actual mother. If Crane's "imaged Word" (which he opposed to T. S. Eliot's "incarnate Word") holds "hushed willows anchored in its glow," then we have a foreshadowing of one of *White Buildings'* most persuasive lyrics, "Repose of Rivers," which tallies the full cost of Crane's confirmation both as poet and as homoerotic quester. Even "The Broken Tower," much closer to Crane's end, is not so profound a self-reading as this river-monologue, in which the river's voice and the poet's own scarcely can be distinguished. The lyric's central stanza subtly repeats, in a finer tone, Whitman's Oedipal trespass in the "Lilacs" elegy, where the precursor-poet merged with the image of the "strong deliveress"—Night, Death, the Mother, and the Sea.

> Lost in the loving floating ocean of thee,
> Laved in the flood of thy bliss O death.

Evading this Whitmanian sublimity, Crane shows a greater hesitation in such a merging:

> How much I would have bartered! The black gorge
> And all the singular nestings in the hills
> Where beavers learn stitch and tooth.
> The pond I entered once and quickly fled—
> I remember now its singing willow rim.

Whitman, who asserted that he dared everything, nevertheless declined tragedy, and died old, just beginning to be honored. Crane gladly would have bartered his tragedy, so as to save a poetic career over at thirty-two, but Crane could live only tragically, unable either to reject his inadequate parents, or to be fully accepted by them. "Quickly fled," and yet not quickly enough, the fascination of "natal power" is hymned by that "singing willow rim," the poet Hart Crane's perpetual music of self-elegy.

5

And yet Crane's genius was Pindaric, as he recognized; what is imperishable in *The Bridge* is not its lyric mourning, but its astonishing transformation of the sublime ode into an American epic, uneven certainly but beyond *The Waste Land* in aspiration and in accomplishment, thus fulfilling Crane's agonistic desire. My critical assertion here would still be disputed by many but time has only freshened the most vital sequences in *The Bridge:*

> You will not hear it as the sea; even stone
> Is not more hushed by gravity . . . But slow,
> As loth to take more tribute—sliding prone
> Like one whose eyes were buried long ago
>
> The River, spreading, flows—and spends your dream.
> What are you, lost within this tideless spell?

At his strongest, Crane rivals Whitman in the intimacy of direct address to the reader, yet more even than Whitman he calls out to lustres that have abandoned the American self. "There was never any more inception than there is now" declares the Emersonian Whitman, but Hart Crane, just seventy years later, asks if he must arrive: "As humbly as a guest who knows himself too late, / His news already told?" At the end of *Song of Myself,* Whitman prophetically had admonished the greatest of the poets to come: "Will you speak before I am gone? Will you prove already too late?" *The Bridge*, knowing its belatedness, still is on fire to affirm, even with the kiss of its poet's agony.

John Irwin has traced Crane's obsession with El Greco's "Agony in the Garden," a painting the poet had worshipped in reproduction for many years before studying it at the National Gallery in London in December 1928. The magnificent Proem, "To Brooklyn Bridge," relies upon El Greco's perspectivism, particularly in the visionary command of spatial relationships:

> *How many dawns, chill from his rippling rest*
> *The seagull's wings shall dip and pivot him,*
> *Shedding white rings of tumult, building high*
> *Over the chained bay waters Liberty—*
>
> *Then, with inviolate curve, forsake our eyes*
> *As apparitional as sails that cross*
> *Some page of figures to be filed away;*
> *—Till elevators drop us from our day . . .*
>
> *I think of cinemas, panoramic sleights*
> *With multitudes bent toward some flashing scene*
> *Never disclosed, but hastened to again,*
> *Foretold to other eyes on the same screen;*
>
> *And Thee, across the harbor, silver-paced*
> *As though the sun took step of thee, yet left*
> *Some motion ever unspent in thy stride,—*
> *Implicitly thy freedom staying thee!*

El Greco's Christ, Irwin observes, kneels in the painting's foreground, staring up at the angel who holds the cup, while imploring God the Father: "Let this cup pass from me" (Matthew 26:39–42). The disciples sleep on the left, while Roman soldiers approach on the right. Higher up on the right is the moon, by whose illumination Christ beholds the cup. Crane's reader stands, as does Crane, with the rising sun at her or his back, beholding Brooklyn Bridge in the dawn's light. The Bridge is at once the cup gazed at by El Greco's Christ and, I would add, William Blake's Sunflower in *Songs of Experience*:

> Ah Sun-flower! weary of time,
> Who countest the steps of the Sun:
> Seeking after that sweet golden clime
> Where the travellers journey is done.

Crane subtly contrasts the Sun-flower, bound into nature, with Brooklyn Bridge—"silver-paced / As though the sun took step of thee, yet left / Some motion ever unspent in thy stride." Yet what is the Bridge's freedom? It is the contrary of the multitude who are entrapped in our modern version of Plato's cave, the "panoramic sleights" of cinema, or of television and computer screens, as Crane would say now. The Bridge's inviolate curve, its superb leap, is the prime image of its freedom, and of the visionary reprieve it grants to its celebrant:

> *O harp and altar, of the fury fused,*
> *(How could mere toil align thy choiring strings!)*
> *Terrific threshold of the prophet's pledge,*
> *Prayer of pariah, and the lover's cry,—*
>
> *Again the traffic lights that skim thy swift*
> *Unfractioned idiom, immaculate sigh of stars,*
> *Beading thy path—condense eternity:*
> *And we have seen night lifted in thine arms.*
>
> *Under thy shadow by the piers I waited;*
> *Only in darkness is thy shadow clear.*
> *The City's fiery parcels all undone,*
> *Already snow submerges an iron year . . .*

O Sleepless as the river under thee,
Vaulting the sea, the prairies' dreaming sod,
Unto us lowliest sometime sweep, descend
And of the curveship lend a myth to God.

The Bridge, both a giant Aeolian harp and the altar of the Unknown God, also suggests a Pietà:

And we have seen night lifted in thine arms.

Crane, more than Whitman, seems to me the poet of the American Religion, questing for a more intimate relationship with God than European dogma affords. Who but Crane could have conceived the magnificent metaphor in which the lights of the Manhattan skyline, seen from the Brooklyn shore at twilight, blaze up into: "The City's fiery parcels all undone," the jagged edges a fiery extension of:

Kiss of our agony Thou gatherest,
O Hand of Fire
gatherest—

The vaulting Bridge, implored to sweep and descend "unto us lowliest," can of its curveship lend a myth not only to God, but to a nation and its handful or fewer of great prophetic poets: Melville, Whitman, Emily Dickinson, Hart Crane. In the early ecstasy of "Atlantis," the authentic origin of his epic, Crane had cried out: "One Song, one Bridge of Fire!" That hardly was to be the poet's ultimate Word, which rends itself apart in "The Broken Tower." But who among our prophets is more eloquent or more central than the Orphic Hart Crane?

6

Hart Crane's tragedy, wholly personal yet also crucial for American poetry, achieves a final perfection in "The Bro-

ken Tower," which vies with "Voyages II," "To Brooklyn
Bridge," and "Repose of Rivers" as Crane's formal master-
work. Widely read in Walter Pater, Crane seems to have en-
countered Pater's beautiful fragment, *Gaston de Latour*.
There, in Chapter I, the young Gaston becomes a clerk in
Holy Orders at his ancestral estate in the southwest region
of La Beauce:

> Seen from the incense-laden sanctuary where the bishop
> was assuming one by one the pontifical ornaments, La Beauce,
> like a many-colored carpet spread under the great dome, with
> the white double house-front quivering afar through the heat,
> though it looked as if you might touch with hand its distant
> spaces, was for a moment the unreal thing. Gaston alone, with
> all his mystic preoccupations, by the privilege of youth,
> seemed to belong to both, and link the visionary company
> about him to the external scene.

Crane beautifully transmuted this into "the visionary
company of love" in a superb quatrain of "The Broken
Tower":

> And so it was I entered the broken world
> To trace the visionary company of love, its voice
> An instant in the wind (I know not whither hurled)
> But not for long to hold each desperate choice.

So central is "The Broken Tower" in poetic tradition that
its "sources" can seem endless, from Dante through Melville
and Pater on to Yeats and to Crane's friend, the poet Léonie
Adams, whose lyric, "Bell Tower," certainly was one of
Crane's starting points. So also was a wonderfully Paterian
sentence in Yeats's reverie, *Per Amica Silentia Lunae* (1917):

> I shall find the dark grow luminous, the void fruitful when
> I understand I have nothing, that the ringers in the tower have
> appointed for the hymen of the soul a passing bell.

"The ringers in the tower" are Crane's "corps / Of shadows in the Tower," the dead precursors who are more outrageously alive than living women and men. Of these, the hidden presence in "The Broken Tower" is Emily Dickinson, who had taught Crane a poetics, as in his quasi-sonnet for her, written in 1927, where she is hailed as the most difficult of American poets, whose "final harvest" requires a reconcilement Crane is yet to attain.

> The harvest you described and understand
> Needs more than wit to gather, love to bind.
> Some reconcilement of remotest mind—

"The Broken Tower," despite its magnificence, rightly doubts that it has achieved Dickinson's stance; too much has been left unreconciled for Crane. The poem catches his desperate, momentary love for Peggy Baird Cowley, his only heterosexual partner, yet it is pervaded also by a nostalgia for a Catholicism he had never known. Crane's own mythic power, his Emersonian heritage of transcendental yearning, knowingly wanes in "The Broken Tower":

> My word I poured. But was it cognate, scored
> Of that tribunal monarch of the air
> Whose thigh embronzes earth, strikes crystal Word
> In wounds pledged once to hope,—cleft to despair?

The poet who had opposed his High Romantic "imaged Word" to the "incarnate word" of T. S. Eliot, seems closer here to Catholic remorse than Eliot ever persuades me *he* is, even in "Ash Wednesday." Crane's "The Broken Tower" could be entitled "Good Friday," and the poet breaks violently with Romantic tradition in his anxiety that his work has been scored by the prince of the powers of the air, Satan.

7

And yet Crane, whose only pragmatic religion was a desperate Self-reliance, could no more have become a Catholic than he could have joined writers on the Left. Ferociously independent, he died still free of faith and of politics, and still bereft of a life-partner or of any profession except poetry. Writing, in 1926, to Waldo Frank, Crane spoke a definitive word upon the place of *The Bridge* in American poetry:

> The form of my poem rises out of a past that so overwhelms the present with its worth and vision that I'm at a loss to explain my delusion that there exist any real links between that past and a future destiny worthy of it. . . . If only America were half as worthy today to be spoken of as Whitman spoke of it fifty years ago there might be something for me to say—

The 1920s, aesthetically productive, nevertheless resemble the 1990s, as an era of emancipated selfishness. Crane had a prophet's sensibility, but suffered the fate of a new Jonah sent against Nineveh, which doubtless repented as we keep repenting, in the American mode of knowing that God loves us. Crane's aspirations remain at least poignant; perhaps some day they could seem more than that. For me, the supreme moment of his poetry abides in the ecstatic celebration of Brooklyn Bridge as a possible knowing or *gnosis,* a music relating to love in harmony and system:

> O Thou steeled Cognizance whose leap commits
> The agile precincts of the lark's return;
> Within whose lariat sweep encinctured sing
> In single chrysalis the many twain,—
> Of stars Thou art the stitch and stallion glow

And like an organ, Thou, with sound of doom—
Sight, sound and flesh Thou leadest from time's realm
As love strikes clear direction for the helm.

That "leap" or "vaulting" is Hart Crane's central metaphor, and as such is his legacy. With Whitman, Dickinson, Frost, Stevens, Eliot—with Emerson also, taking his prose and poetry together—Crane is in the central line of American poetic achievement. Since Crane's death, there have been a few more of that eminence: Elizabeth Bishop, Ammons, Ashbery, Merrill, and there are younger poets who may attain that height. I return here, as I close, to our loss. Hart Crane, at thirty-two, leapt into the sea evidently because he had concluded that his poetic gift had died already. Tragically mistaken, he torments his admirers at this, his centenary, with speculations upon the poems they have lost.

Acknowledgments

I wish to acknowledge Victor Schmalzer for his sponsorship of this reader's edition of Hart Crane's poems, and David Mann for granting his authorization.

My greatest debt, incurred during countless hours while working among the largest collection of Hart Crane materials, which is housed in the Butler Library of Columbia University, is owed to Kenneth A. Lohf. Without his hospitality and extraordinary help, and the cooperation of his staff (Bernard Cristal, Mary Bolin, and Henry Rowen in particular) this edition could have never been done. I am grateful for all their patient aid. I am pleased to acknowledge the Hart Crane Papers, Rare Book and Manuscript Library, Columbia University, for permission to publish extensively from the material in their collection.

Donald Gallup and the staff at The Beinecke Library, Yale University, made my many visits a pleasure, which I acknowledge with happiest memories. Richard W. Oram was always helpful when I needed detailed information regarding Crane's proofs for the New York edition of *THE BRIDGE*, which are housed at the Harry Ransom Humanities Research Center, The University of Texas at Austin, whose staff—Sally Leach and Ellen S. Dunlap especially—were most helpful in response to my many queries. For permission to publish "After Jonah," "Supplication to the Muses . . . ," and for use of the proofs of *THE BRIDGE* and *White Buildings* I acknowledge the Harry Ransom Humanities Research Center. I thank them, and also Robert A. Tibbetts (and his predecessor Richard A. Ploch) of The Ohio State University Libraries for their similar help regarding the documents of four poems in the Gorham Munson Collection that are the basis for those texts in this edition, and for their constant support whenever I needed answers to questions regarding their Hart Crane documents. I gratefully acknowledge The Ohio State University Libraries for permission to publish the versions of "The Bridge of Estador," "Episode of Hands," "Porphyro in Akron," and "What Nots ?" which are in their Special Collections.

Neda M. Westlake and her staff of the University of Pennsylvania Rare Book Collection were very helpful whenever I was in need, especially concerning "Euclid Avenue" and "O Moon, Thou Cool . . ." in the Waldo Frank Collection, Department of Special Collections, Van Pelt Library, University of Pennsylvania, which I gratefully acknowledge for permission to publish those two works. To the Fisk University Library staff goes my gratitude for their help with Hart Crane materials in the Jean Toomer Collection. Rosemary L. Cullen of the Harris Collection in the Brown University Library was likewise helpful regarding "Of an Evening. . . ." I wish to acknowledge the Brown University Library for permission to publish that poem in this edition. To all the above I extend my sincerest thanks, for without their cooperation and support this reader's edition could not be published.

The following institutions and their library staffs I also wish to thank for their many courtesies regarding Hart Crane holdings: Southern Illinois University Library; The Bancroft Library, University of California, Berkeley; Princeton University Library; Kent State University Library; The University of Chicago Library; Syracuse University Library; The Pennsylvania State University Libraries, University Park; University of Virginia Library; University of Maryland Library; Oral History Research Project of Columbia University; Archives of American Art of the Smithsonian Institution; Georgetown University Library; Indiana University Library; Harvard University Library; Lockwood Memorial Library of the State University of New York at Buffalo; University of Delaware Library; University of Wisconsin Library, Milwaukee; The Center for Research Libraries; Oberlin College Library; The University of Wyoming Divison of Rare Books and Special Collections; Marquette University Memorial Library

Archives; State University of New York at Stony Brook Library; the University of California Library, Davis; Hamilton College Library; Library of the Whitney Museum of Art; and the Pierpont Morgan Library. Irena Murray and John Black of McGill University Libraries were particularly helpful, as was the McGill Libraries staff generally, along with the reference departments of The New York Public Library, Free Library of Philadelphia at Logan Square, and Côte St. Luc Public Library.

Special thanks for their careful attention to my inquiries go to Brom Weber, Philip Horton, David V. Koch, Kenneth W. Duckett, Philip Kaplan, Joan St.C. Crane, Hilary Cummings, Anne Freudenberg, Mary Bocaccio, Dean Keller, James D. Hart, Fredson T. Bowers, Maurice F. Neville, James Pepper, Stanley Mallach, Herbert Cahoon, George M. Barringer, John S. Mayfield, Charles W. Mann, Lola Szladits, Brian McInerney, Stuart Dick, Arna Bontemps, Beth M. Howse, Ann Allen Schockley, Sue Chandler, Mary E. Cowles, Elizabeth Stege Teleky, Margaret McFadden, Jean F. Preston, Mary Ann Jensen, May FitzGerald, Mrs. William Wright, Mrs. Charles Harris, William Slater Brown, Malcolm Cowley, Dennis L. Read, Peter Blume, John Unterecker, Don L. Cook, David W. Swetland, Peter Dwonzkowski, David E. Schoonover, Robert C. Schweik, Joseph Schwartz, Joe Erdelac, Vivian Pemberton, K. C. Gay, Eric Carpenter, Leonard B. Schlosser, Daniel L. Winters, Esther Kelley, Pat McDonnell, Charles B. Elston, Jean Seegraber, John C. Broderick, Evert Volkersz, Frank K. Lorenz and Carolyn Ann Davis.

For helping to make this reader's edition possible, I wish to express my appreciation to Gay Wilson Allen, Herbert Leibowitz, R. W. B. Lewis, Hershel Parker, Allen Grossman, Thomas F. Parkinson, Margaret Dickie, Carol Stiles, John Benedict, Pamela Long, Daniel and Carla Saykaly, and Anthony Sisti.

My warm thanks for generous hospitality and support of the research which helped make this edition a reality go to Robert K. Martin, Thomas S. W. Lewis, William C. Wees, Warren Herendeen, Donald G. Parker, Janet Lewis Winters, Mr. and Mrs.

Richard W. Rychtarik, Mr. and Mrs. Carl Schmitt and family, Brian Robinson, Arthur Broes, Belle Simon, Jeanne Blumberg, Mr. and Mrs. Harvey S. Cohen, Esq.; Bruce D. Cohen, Esq.; and Don Black.

For grants in aid of the research that has brought this project to fruition, I wish to thank the American Philosophical Society, the McGill University Department of English and Faculty of Graduate Studies, and the Social Sciences and Humanities Research Council of Canada.

My deepest thanks go to Evelyn M. B. Simon for her constant assistance and support.

October 1985   Marc Simon

WHITE BUILDINGS

Ce ne peut être que la fin du monde, en avançant.
—RIMBAUD

LEGEND

As silent as a mirror is believed
Realities plunge in silence by . . .

I am not ready for repentance;
Nor to match regrets. For the moth
Bends no more than the still
Imploring flame. And tremorous
In the white falling flakes
Kisses are,—
The only worth all granting.

It is to be learned—
This cleaving and this burning,
But only by the one who
Spends out himself again.

Twice and twice
(Again the smoking souvenir,
Bleeding eidolon!) and yet again.
Until the bright logic is won
Unwhispering as a mirror
Is believed.

Then, drop by caustic drop, a perfect cry
Shall string some constant harmony,—
Relentless caper for all those who step
The legend of their youth into the noon.

BLACK TAMBOURINE

The interests of a black man in a cellar
Mark tardy judgment on the world's closed door.
Gnats toss in the shadow of a bottle,
And a roach spans a crevice in the floor.

5   Aesop, driven to pondering, found
Heaven with the tortoise and the hare;
Fox brush and sow ear top his grave
And mingling incantations on the air.

The black man, forlorn in the cellar,
10   Wanders in some mid-kingdom, dark, that lies,
Between his tambourine, stuck on the wall,
And, in Africa, a carcass quick with flies.

EMBLEMS OF CONDUCT

By a peninsula the wanderer sat and sketched
The uneven valley graves. While the apostle gave
Alms to the meek the volcano burst
With sulphur and aureate rocks . . .
5   For joy rides in stupendous coverings
Luring the living into spiritual gates.

Orators follow the universe
And radio the complete laws to the people.
The apostle conveys thought through discipline.
10   Bowls and cups fill historians with adorations,—
Dull lips commemorating spiritual gates.

The wanderer later chose this spot of rest
Where marble clouds support the sea
And where was finally borne a chosen hero.
15   By that time summer and smoke were past.
Dolphins still played, arching the horizons,
But only to build memories of spiritual gates.

MY GRANDMOTHER'S LOVE LETTERS

There are no stars tonight
But those of memory.
Yet how much room for memory there is
In the loose girdle of soft rain.

5   There is even room enough
For the letters of my mother's mother,
Elizabeth,
That have been pressed so long
Into a corner of the roof
10   That they are brown and soft,
And liable to melt as snow.

Over the greatness of such space
Steps must be gentle.
It is all hung by an invisible white hair.
15   It trembles as birch limbs webbing the air.

And I ask myself:

"Are your fingers long enough to play
Old keys that are but echoes:
Is the silence strong enough
20   To carry back the music to its source
And back to you again
As though to her?"

Yet I would lead my grandmother by the hand
Through much of what she would not understand;
25   And so I stumble. And the rain continues on the roof
With such a sound of gently pitying laughter.

SUNDAY MORNING APPLES

To William Sommer

The leaves will fall again sometime and fill
The fleece of nature with those purposes
That are your rich and faithful strength of line.

But now there are challenges to spring
In that ripe nude with head
                       reared
Into a realm of swords, her purple shadow
Bursting on the winter of the world
From whiteness that cries defiance to the snow.

A boy runs with a dog before the sun, straddling
Spontaneities that form their independent orbits,
Their own perennials of light
In the valley where you live
                      (called Brandywine).

I have seen the apples there that toss you secrets,—
Beloved apples of seasonable madness
That feed your inquiries with aerial wine.
Put them again beside a pitcher with a knife,
And poise them full and ready for explosion—
The apples, Bill, the apples!

PRAISE FOR AN URN

In Memoriam: Ernest Nelson

It was a kind and northern face
That mingled in such exile guise
The everlasting eyes of Pierrot
And, of Gargantua, the laughter.

5   His thoughts, delivered to me
From the white coverlet and pillow,
I see now, were inheritances—
Delicate riders of the storm.

The slant moon on the slanting hill
10   Once moved us toward presentiments
Of what the dead keep, living still,
And such assessments of the soul

As, perched in the crematory lobby,
The insistent clock commented on,
15   Touching as well upon our praise
Of glories proper to the time.

Still, having in mind gold hair,
I cannot see that broken brow
And miss the dry sound of bees
20   Stretching across a lucid space.

Scatter these well-meant idioms
Into the smoky spring that fills
The suburbs, where they will be lost.
They are no trophies of the sun.

GARDEN ABSTRACT

The apple on its bough is her desire,—
Shining suspension, mimic of the sun.
The bough has caught her breath up, and her voice,
Dumbly articulate in the slant and rise
Of branch on branch above her, blurs her eyes.
She is prisoner of the tree and its green fingers.

And so she comes to dream herself the tree,
The wind possessing her, weaving her young veins,
Holding her to the sky and its quick blue,
Drowning the fever of her hands in sunlight.
She has no memory, nor fear, nor hope
Beyond the grass and shadows at her feet.

STARK MAJOR

The lover's death, how regular
With lifting spring and starker
Vestiges of the sun that somehow
Filter in to us before we waken.

5   Not yet is there that heat and sober
Vivisection of more clamant air
That hands joined in the dark will answer
After the daily circuits of its glare.

It is the time of sundering . . .
10 Beneath the green silk counterpane
Her mound of undelivered life
Lies cool upon her—not yet pain.

And she will wake before you pass,
Scarcely aloud, beyond her door,
15 And every third step down the stair
Until you reach the muffled floor—

Will laugh and call your name; while you,
Still answering her faint good-byes,
Will find the street, only to look
20 At doors and stone with broken eyes.

Walk now, and note the lover's death.
Henceforth her memory is more
Than yours, in cries, in ecstasies
You cannot ever reach to share.

CHAPLINESQUE

We make our meek adjustments,
Contented with such random consolations
As the wind deposits
In slithered and too ample pockets.

5   For we can still love the world, who find
A famished kitten on the step, and know
Recesses for it from the fury of the street,
Or warm torn elbow coverts.

We will sidestep, and to the final smirk
10   Dally the doom of that inevitable thumb
That slowly chafes its puckered index toward us,
Facing the dull squint with what innocence
And what surprise!

And yet these fine collapses are not lies
15   More than the pirouettes of any pliant cane;
Our obsequies are, in a way, no enterprise.
We can evade you, and all else but the heart:
What blame to us if the heart live on.

The game enforces smirks; but we have seen
20   The moon in lonely alleys make
A grail of laughter of an empty ash can,
And through all sound of gaiety and quest
Have heard a kitten in the wilderness.

PASTORALE

No more violets,
And the year
Broken into smoky panels.
What woods remember now
5   Her calls, her enthusiasms.

That ritual of sap and leaves
The sun drew out,
Ends in this latter muffled
Bronze and brass. The wind
10   Takes rein.

If, dusty, I bear
An image beyond this
Already fallen harvest,
I can only query, "Fool—
15   Have you remembered too long;

Or was there too little said
For ease or resolution—
Summer scarcely begun
And violets,
20   A few picked, the rest dead?"

IN SHADOW

Out in the late amber afternoon,
Confused among chrysanthemums,
Her parasol, a pale balloon,
Like a waiting moon, in shadow swims.

5   Her furtive lace and misty hair
Over the garden dial distill
The sunlight,—then withdrawing, wear
Again the shadows at her will.

Gently yet suddenly, the sheen
10 Of stars inwraps her parasol.
She hears my step behind the green
Twilight, stiller than shadows, fall.

"Come, it is too late,—too late
To risk alone the light's decline:
15 Nor has the evening long to wait,"—
But her own words are night's and mine.

THE FERNERY

The lights that travel on her spectacles
Seldom, now, meet a mirror in her eyes.
But turning, as you may chance to lift a shade
Beside her and her fernery, is to follow
5   The zigzags fast around dry lips composed
To darkness through a wreath of sudden pain.

—So, while fresh sunlight splinters humid green
I have known myself a nephew to confusions
That sometimes take up residence and reign
10   In crowns less grey—O merciless tidy hair!

NORTH LABRADOR

A land of leaning ice
Hugged by plaster-grey arches of sky,
Flings itself silently
Into eternity.

5   "Has no one come here to win you,
Or left you with the faintest blush
Upon your glittering breasts?
Have you no memories, O Darkly Bright?"

Cold-hushed, there is only the shifting of moments
10   That journey toward no Spring—
No birth, no death, no time nor sun
In answer.

REPOSE OF RIVERS

The willows carried a slow sound,
A sarabande the wind mowed on the mead.
I could never remember
That seething, steady leveling of the marshes
5 Till age had brought me to the sea.

Flags, weeds. And remembrance of steep alcoves
Where cypresses shared the noon's
Tyranny; they drew me into hades almost.
And mammoth turtles climbing sulphur dreams
10 Yielded, while sun-silt rippled them
Asunder . . .

How much I would have bartered! the black gorge
And all the singular nestings in the hills
Where beavers learn stitch and tooth.
15 The pond I entered once and quickly fled—
I remember now its singing willow rim.

And finally, in that memory all things nurse;
After the city that I finally passed
With scalding unguents spread and smoking darts
20 The monsoon cut across the delta
At gulf gates . . . There, beyond the dykes

I heard wind flaking sapphire, like this summer,
And willows could not hold more steady sound.

PARAPHRASE

Of a steady winking beat between
Systole, diastole spokes-of-a-wheel
One rushing from the bed at night
May find the record wedged in his soul.

5   Above the feet the clever sheets
Lie guard upon the integers of life:
For what skims in between uncurls the toe,
Involves the hands in purposeless repose.

But from its bracket how can the tongue tell
10   When systematic morn shall sometime flood
The pillow—how desperate is the light
That shall not rouse, how faint the crow's cavil

As, when stunned in that antarctic blaze,
Your head, unrocking to a pulse, already
15   Hollowed by air, posts a white paraphrase
Among bruised roses on the papered wall.

POSSESSIONS

Witness now this trust! the rain
That steals softly direction
And the key, ready to hand—sifting
One moment in sacrifice (the direst)
5   Through a thousand nights the flesh
Assaults outright for bolts that linger
Hidden,—O undirected as the sky
That through its black foam has no eyes
For this fixed stone of lust . . .

10   Accumulate such moments to an hour:
Account the total of this trembling tabulation.
I know the screen, the distant flying taps
And stabbing medley that sways—
And the mercy, feminine, that stays
15   As though prepared.

And I, entering, take up the stone
As quiet as you can make a man . . .
In Bleecker Street, still trenchant in a void,
Wounded by apprehensions out of speech,
20   I hold it up against a disk of light—
I, turning, turning on smoked forking spires,
The city's stubborn lives, desires.

Tossed on these horns, who bleeding dies,
Lacks all but piteous admissions to be spilt
25   Upon the page whose blind sum finally burns
Record of rage and partial appetites.
The pure possession, the inclusive cloud
Whose heart is fire shall come,—the white wind rase
All but bright stones wherein our smiling plays.

LACHRYMAE CHRISTI

Whitely, while benzine
Rinsings from the moon
Dissolve all but the windows of the mills
(Inside the sure machinery
5   Is still
And curdled only where a sill
Sluices its one unyielding smile)

Immaculate venom binds
The fox's teeth, and swart
10   Thorns freshen on the year's
First blood. From flanks unfended,
Twanged red perfidies of spring
Are trillion on the hill.

And the nights opening
15   Chant pyramids,—
Anoint with innocence,—recall
To music and retrieve what perjuries
Had galvanized the eyes.

                While chime
20   Beneath and all around
Distilling clemencies,—worms'
Inaudible whistle, tunneling
Not penitence
But song, as these
25   Perpetual fountains, vines,—

Thy Nazarene and tinder eyes.

(Let sphinxes from the ripe
Borage of death have cleared my tongue
Once and again; vermin and rod

30   No longer bind. Some sentient cloud
        Of tears flocks through the tendoned loam:
        Betrayed stones slowly speak.)

        Names peeling from Thine eyes
        And their undimming lattices of flame,
35   Spell out in palm and pain
        Compulsion of the year, O Nazarene.

        Lean long from sable, slender boughs,
        Unstanched and luminous. And as the nights
        Strike from Thee perfect spheres,
40   Lift up in lilac-emerald breath the grail
        Of earth again—

                    Thy face
        From charred and riven stakes, O
        Dionysus, Thy
45   Unmangled target smile.

PASSAGE

Where the cedar leaf divides the sky
I heard the sea.
In sapphire arenas of the hills
I was promised an improved infancy.

5 Sulking, sanctioning the sun,
My memory I left in a ravine,—
Casual louse that tissues the buckwheat,
Aprons rocks, congregates pears
In moonlit bushels
10 And wakens alleys with a hidden cough.

Dangerously the summer burned
(I had joined the entrainments of the wind).
The shadows of boulders lengthened my back:
In the bronze gongs of my cheeks
15 The rain dried without odour.

"It is not long, it is not long;
See where the red and black
Vine-stanchioned valleys—": but the wind
Died speaking through the ages that you know
20 And hug, chimney-sooted heart of man!
So was I turned about and back, much as your smoke
Compiles a too well known biography.

The evening was a spear in the ravine
That throve through very oak. And had I walked
25 The dozen particular decimals of time?
Touching an opening laurel, I found
A thief beneath, my stolen book in hand.

"Why are you back here—smiling an iron coffin?"
"To argue with the laurel," I replied:

30   "Am justified in transience, fleeing
Under the constant wonder of your eyes—."

He closed the book. And from the Ptolemies
Sand troughed us in a glittering abyss.
A serpent swam a vertex to the sun
35   —On unpaced beaches leaned its tongue and drummed.
What fountains did I hear? what icy speeches?
Memory, committed to the page, had broke.

THE WINE MENAGERIE

Invariably when wine redeems the sight,
Narrowing the mustard scansions of the eyes,
A leopard ranging always in the brow
Asserts a vision in the slumbering gaze.

5 Then glozening decanters that reflect the street
Wear me in crescents on their bellies. Slow
Applause flows into liquid cynosures:
—I am conscripted to their shadows' glow.

Against the imitation onyx wainscoting
10 (Painted emulsion of snow, eggs, yarn, coal, manure)
Regard the forceps of the smile that takes her.
Percussive sweat is spreading to his hair. Mallets,
Her eyes, unmake an instant of the world . . .

What is it in this heap the serpent pries—
15 Whose skin, facsimile of time, unskeins
Octagon, sapphire transepts round the eyes;
—From whom some whispered carillon assures
Speed to the arrow into feathered skies?

Sharp to the windowpane guile drags a face,
20 And as the alcove of her jealousy recedes
An urchin who has left the snow
Nudges a cannister across the bar
While August meadows somewhere clasp his brow.

Each chamber, transept, coins some squint,
25 Remorseless line, minting their separate wills—
Poor streaked bodies wreathing up and out,
Unwitting the stigma that each turn repeals:
Between black tusks the roses shine!

23

New thresholds, new anatomies! Wine talons
30   Build freedom up about me and distill
This competence—to travel in a tear
Sparkling alone, within another's will.

Until my blood dreams a receptive smile
Wherein new purities are snared; where chimes
35   Before some flame of gaunt repose a shell
Tolled once, perhaps, by every tongue in hell.
—Anguished, the wit that cries out of me:

"Alas,—these frozen billows of your skill!
Invent new dominoes of love and bile . . .
40   Ruddy, the tooth implicit of the world
Has followed you. Though in the end you know
And count some dim inheritance of sand,
How much yet meets the treason of the snow.

"Rise from the dates and crumbs. And walk away,
45   Stepping over Holofernes' shins—
Beyond the wall, whose severed head floats by
With Baptist John's. Their whispering begins.

"—And fold your exile on your back again;
Petrushka's valentine pivots on its pin."

RECITATIVE

Regard the capture here, O Janus-faced,
As double as the hands that twist this glass.
Such eyes at search or rest you cannot see;
Reciting pain or glee, how can you bear!

5 Twin shadowed halves: the breaking second holds
In each the skin alone, and so it is
I crust a plate of vibrant mercury
Borne cleft to you, and brother in the half.

Inquire this much-exacting fragment smile,
10 Its drums and darkest blowing leaves ignore,—
Defer though, revocation of the tears
That yield attendance to one crucial sign.

Look steadily—how the wind feasts and spins
The brain's disk shivered against lust. Then watch
15 While darkness, like an ape's face, falls away,
And gradually white buildings answer day.

Let the same nameless gulf beleaguer us—
Alike suspend us from atrocious sums
Built floor by floor on shafts of steel that grant
20 The plummet heart, like Absalom, no stream.

The highest tower,—let her ribs palisade
Wrenched gold of Nineveh;—yet leave the tower.
The bridge swings over salvage, beyond wharves;
A wind abides the ensign of your will . . .

25 In alternating bells have you not heard
All hours clapped dense into a single stride?
Forgive me for an echo of these things,
And let us walk through time with equal pride.

25

FOR THE MARRIAGE OF FAUSTUS AND HELEN

> *"And so we may arrive by Talmud skill*
> *And profane Greek to raise the building up*
> *Of Helen's house against the Ismaelite,*
> *King of Thogarma, and his habergeons*
> *Brimstony, blue and fiery; and the force*
> *Of King Abaddon, and the beast of Cittim;*
> *Which Rabbi David Kimchi, Onkelos,*
> *And Aben Ezra do interpret Rome."*
>
> —THE ALCHEMIST.

I

The mind has shown itself at times
Too much the baked and labeled dough
Divided by accepted multitudes.
Across the stacked partitions of the day—
5   Across the memoranda, baseball scores,
The stenographic smiles and stock quotations
Smutty wings flash out equivocations.

The mind is brushed by sparrow wings;
Numbers, rebuffed by asphalt, crowd
10   The margins of the day, accent the curbs,
Convoying divers dawns on every corner
To druggist, barber and tobacconist,
Until the graduate opacities of evening
Take them away as suddenly to somewhere
15   Virginal perhaps, less fragmentary, cool.

> *There is the world dimensional for*
> *those untwisted by the love of things*
> *irreconcilable . . .*

And yet, suppose some evening I forgot
20   The fare and transfer, yet got by that way
Without recall,—lost yet poised in traffic.

Then I might find your eyes across an aisle,
Still flickering with those prefigurations—
Prodigal, yet uncontested now,
25 Half-riant before the jerky window frame.

There is some way, I think, to touch
Those hands of yours that count the nights
Stippled with pink and green advertisements.
And now, before its arteries turn dark
30 I would have you meet this bartered blood.
Imminent in his dream, none better knows
The white wafer cheek of love, or offers words
Lightly as moonlight on the eaves meets snow.

Reflective conversion of all things
35 At your deep blush, when ecstasies thread
The limbs and belly, when rainbows spread
Impinging on the throat and sides . . .
Inevitable, the body of the world
Weeps in inventive dust for the hiatus
40 That winks above it, bluet in your breasts.

The earth may glide diaphanous to death;
But if I lift my arms it is to bend
To you who turned away once, Helen, knowing
The press of troubled hands, too alternate
45 With steel and soil to hold you endlessly.
I meet you, therefore, in that eventual flame
You found in final chains, no captive then—
Beyond their million brittle, bloodshot eyes;
White, through white cities passed on to assume
50 That world which comes to each of us alone.

Accept a lone eye riveted to your plane,
Bent axle of devotion along companion ways
That beat, continuous, to hourless days—
One inconspicuous, glowing orb of praise.

II

Brazen hypnotics glitter here;
Glee shifts from foot to foot,
Magnetic to their tremulo.
This crashing opéra bouffe,
5 Blest excursion! this ricochet
From roof to roof—
Know, Olympians, we are breathless
While nigger cupids scour the stars!

A thousand light shrugs balance us
10 Through snarling hails of melody.
White shadows slip across the floor
Splayed like cards from a loose hand;
Rhythmic ellipses lead into canters
Until somewhere a rooster banters.

15 Greet naïvely—yet intrepidly
New soothings, new amazements
That cornets introduce at every turn—
And you may fall downstairs with me
With perfect grace and equanimity.
20 Or, plaintively scud past shores
Where, by strange harmonic laws
All relatives, serene and cool,
Sit rocked in patent armchairs.

O, I have known metallic paradises
25 Where cuckoos clucked to finches
Above the deft catastrophes of drums.
While titters hailed the groans of death
Beneath gyrating awnings I have seen

The incunabula of the divine grotesque.
30   This music has a reassuring way.

The siren of the springs of guilty song—
Let us take her on the incandescent wax
Striated with nuances, nervosities
That we are heir to: she is still so young,
35   We cannot frown upon her as she smiles,
Dipping here in this cultivated storm
Among slim skaters of the gardened skies.

III

Capped arbiter of beauty in this street
That narrows darkly into motor dawn,—
You, here beside me, delicate ambassador
Of intricate slain numbers that arise
5   In whispers, naked of steel;
                    religious gunman!
Who faithfully, yourself, will fall too soon,
And in other ways than as the wind settles
On the sixteen thrifty bridges of the city:
10 Let us unbind our throats of fear and pity.

                    We even,
Who drove speediest destruction
In corymbulous formations of mechanics,—
Who hurried the hill breezes, spouting malice
15 Plangent over meadows, and looked down
On rifts of torn and empty houses
Like old women with teeth unjubilant
That waited faintly, briefly and in vain:

We know, eternal gunman, our flesh remembers
20 The tensile boughs, the nimble blue plateaus,
The mounted, yielding cities of the air!

That saddled sky that shook down vertical
Repeated play of fire—no hypogeum
Of wave or rock was good against one hour.
25 We did not ask for that, but have survived,
And will persist to speak again before
All stubble streets that have not curved
To memory, or known the ominous lifted arm

That lowers down the arc of Helen's brow
30   To saturate with blessing and dismay.

A goose, tobacco and cologne—
Three winged and gold-shod prophecies of heaven,
The lavish heart shall always have to leaven
And spread with bells and voices, and atone
35   The abating shadows of our conscript dust.

Anchises' navel, dripping of the sea,—
The hands Erasmus dipped in gleaming tides,
Gathered the voltage of blown blood and vine;
Delve upward for the new and scattered wine,
40   O brother-thief of time, that we recall.
Laugh out the meager penance of their days
Who dare not share with us the breath released,
The substance drilled and spent beyond repair
For golden, or the shadow of gold hair.

45   Distinctly praise the years, whose volatile
Blamed bleeding hands extend and thresh the height
The imagination spans beyond despair,
Outpacing bargain, vocable and prayer.

AT MELVILLE'S TOMB

Often beneath the wave, wide from this ledge
The dice of drowned men's bones he saw bequeath
An embassy. Their numbers as he watched,
Beat on the dusty shore and were obscured.

And wrecks passed without sound of bells,
The calyx of death's bounty giving back
A scattered chapter, livid hieroglyph,
The portent wound in corridors of shells.

Then in the circuit calm of one vast coil,
Its lashings charmed and malice reconciled,
Frosted eyes there were that lifted altars;
And silent answers crept across the stars.

Compass, quadrant and sextant contrive
No farther tides . . . High in the azure steeps
Monody shall not wake the mariner.
This fabulous shadow only the sea keeps.

VOYAGES

Above the fresh ruffles of the surf
Bright striped urchins flay each other with sand.
They have contrived a conquest for shell shucks,
And their fingers crumble fragments of baked weed
5   Gaily digging and scattering.

And in answer to their treble interjections
The sun beats lightning on the waves,
The waves fold thunder on the sand;
And could they hear me I would tell them:

10 O brilliant kids, frisk with your dog,
Fondle your shells and sticks, bleached
By time and the elements; but there is a line
You must not cross nor ever trust beyond it
Spry cordage of your bodies to caresses
15 Too lichen-faithful from too wide a breast.
The bottom of the sea is cruel.

II

—And yet this great wink of eternity,
Of rimless floods, unfettered leewardings,
Samite sheeted and processioned where
Her undinal vast belly moonward bends,
5   Laughing the wrapt inflections of our love;

Take this Sea, whose diapason knells
On scrolls of silver snowy sentences,
The sceptred terror of whose sessions rends
As her demeanors motion well or ill,
10 All but the pieties of lovers' hands.

And onward, as bells off San Salvador
Salute the crocus lustres of the stars,
In these poinsettia meadows of her tides,—
Adagios of islands, O my Prodigal,
15 Complete the dark confessions her veins spell.

Mark how her turning shoulders wind the hours,
And hasten while her penniless rich palms
Pass superscription of bent foam and wave,—
Hasten, while they are true,—sleep, death, desire,
20 Close round one instant in one floating flower.

Bind us in time, O Seasons clear, and awe.
O minstrel galleons of Carib fire,
Bequeath us to no earthly shore until
Is answered in the vortex of our grave
25 The seal's wide spindrift gaze toward paradise.

III

Infinite consanguinity it bears—
This tendered theme of you that light
Retrieves from sea plains where the sky
Resigns a breast that every wave enthrones;
5   While ribboned water lanes I wind
Are laved and scattered with no stroke
Wide from your side, whereto this hour
The sea lifts, also, reliquary hands.

And so, admitted through black swollen gates
10   That must arrest all distance otherwise,—
Past whirling pillars and lithe pediments,
Light wrestling there incessantly with light,
Star kissing star through wave on wave unto
Your body rocking!
15   and where death, if shed,
Presumes no carnage, but this single change,—
Upon the steep floor flung from dawn to dawn
The silken skilled transmemberment of song;

Permit me voyage, love, into your hands . . .

IV

Whose counted smile of hours and days, suppose
I know as spectrum of the sea and pledge
Vastly now parting gulf on gulf of wings
Whose circles bridge, I know, (from palms to the severe
5   Chilled albatross's white immutability)
No stream of greater love advancing now
Than, singing, this mortality alone
Through clay aflow immortally to you.

All fragrance irrefragably, and claim
10 Madly meeting logically in this hour
And region that is ours to wreathe again,
Portending eyes and lips and making told
The chancel port and portion of our June—

Shall they not stem and close in our own steps
15 Bright staves of flowers and quills today as I
Must first be lost in fatal tides to tell?

In signature of the incarnate word
The harbor shoulders to resign in mingling
Mutual blood, transpiring as foreknown
20 And widening noon within your breast for gathering
All bright insinuations that my years have caught
For islands where must lead inviolably
Blue latitudes and levels of your eyes,—

In this expectant, still exclaim receive
25 The secret oar and petals of all love.

V

Meticulous, past midnight in clear rime,
Infrangible and lonely, smooth as though cast
Together in one merciless white blade—
The bay estuaries fleck the hard sky limits.

5   —As if too brittle or too clear to touch!
The cables of our sleep so swiftly filed,
Already hang, shred ends from remembered stars.
One frozen trackless smile . . . What words
Can strangle this deaf moonlight? For we

10 Are overtaken. Now no cry, no sword
Can fasten or deflect this tidal wedge,
Slow tyranny of moonlight, moonlight loved
And changed . . . "There's

Nothing like this in the world," you say,
15 Knowing I cannot touch your hand and look
Too, into that godless cleft of sky
Where nothing turns but dead sands flashing.

"—And never to quite understand!" No,
In all the argosy of your bright hair I dreamed
20 Nothing so flagless as this piracy.

But now
Draw in your head, alone and too tall here.
Your eyes already in the slant of drifting foam;
Your breath sealed by the ghosts I do not know:
25 Draw in your head and sleep the long way home.

VI

Where icy and bright dungeons lift
Of swimmers their lost morning eyes,
And ocean rivers, churning, shift
Green borders under stranger skies,

5   Steadily as a shell secretes
Its beating leagues of monotone,
Or as many waters trough the sun's
Red kelson past the cape's wet stone;

O rivers mingling toward the sky
10 And harbor of the phoenix' breast—
My eyes pressed black against the prow,
—Thy derelict and blinded guest

Waiting, afire, what name, unspoke,
I cannot claim: let thy waves rear
15 More savage than the death of kings,
Some splintered garland for the seer.

Beyond siroccos harvesting
The solstice thunders, crept away,
Like a cliff swinging or a sail
20 Flung into April's inmost day—

Creation's blithe and petalled word
To the lounged goddess when she rose
Conceding dialogue with eyes
That smile unsearchable repose—

25 Still fervid covenant, Belle Isle,
—Unfolded floating dais before

Which rainbows twine continual hair—
Belle Isle, white echo of the oar!

The imaged Word, it is, that holds
30 Hushed willows anchored in its glow.
It is the unbetrayable reply
Whose accent no farewell can know.

THE BRIDGE

From going to and fro in the earth,
and from walking up and down in it.
THE BOOK OF JOB

TO
BROOKLYN BRIDGE

How many dawns, chill from his rippling rest
The seagull's wings shall dip and pivot him,
Shedding white rings of tumult, building high
Over the chained bay waters Liberty—

5   *Then, with inviolate curve, forsake our eyes*
As apparitional as sails that cross
Some page of figures to be filed away;
—Till elevators drop us from our day . . .

I think of cinemas, panoramic sleights
10 *With multitudes bent toward some flashing scene*
Never disclosed, but hastened to again,
Foretold to other eyes on the same screen;

And Thee, across the harbor, silver-paced
As though the sun took step of thee, yet left
15 *Some motion ever unspent in thy stride,—*
Implicitly thy freedom staying thee!

Out of some subway scuttle, cell or loft
A bedlamite speeds to thy parapets,
Tilting there momently, shrill shirt ballooning,
20 *A jest falls from the speechless caravan.*

Down Wall, from girder into street noon leaks,
A rip-tooth of the sky's acetylene;
All afternoon the cloud-flown derricks turn . . .
Thy cables breathe the North Atlantic still.

25 *And obscure as that heaven of the Jews,*
Thy guerdon . . . Accolade thou dost bestow

Of anonymity time cannot raise:
Vibrant reprieve and pardon thou dost show.

O harp and altar, of the fury fused,
30   *(How could mere toil align thy choiring strings!)*
Terrific threshold of the prophet's pledge,
Prayer of pariah, and the lover's cry,—

Again the traffic lights that skim thy swift
Unfractioned idiom, immaculate sigh of stars,
35   *Beading thy path—condense eternity:*
And we have seen night lifted in thine arms.

Under thy shadow by the piers I waited;
Only in darkness is thy shadow clear.
The City's fiery parcels all undone,
40   *Already snow submerges an iron year . . .*

O Sleepless as the river under thee,
Vaulting the sea, the prairies' dreaming sod,
Unto us lowliest sometime sweep, descend
And of the curveship lend a myth to God.

I
AVE MARIA

Venient annis, saecula seris,
Quibus Oceanus vincula rerum
Laxet et ingens pateat tellus
Tethysque novos detegat orbes
Nec sit terris ultima Thule.

—SENECA

AVE MARIA

Be with me, Luis de San Angel, now—
Witness before the tides can wrest away
The word I bring, O you who reined my suit
Into the Queen's great heart that doubtful day;
For I have seen now what no perjured breath
Of clown nor sage can riddle or gainsay;—
To you, too, Juan Perez, whose counsel fear
And greed adjourned,—I bring you back Cathay!

Columbus, alone, gazing toward Spain, invokes the presence of two faithful partisans of his quest . . .

Here waves climb into dusk on gleaming mail;
Invisible valves of the sea,—locks, tendons
Crested and creeping, troughing corridors
That fall back yawning to another plunge.
Slowly the sun's red caravel drops light
Once more behind us. . . . It is morning there—
O where our Indian emperies lie revealed,
Yet lost, all, let this keel one instant yield!

I thought of Genoa; and this truth, now proved,
That made me exile in her streets, stood me
More absolute than ever—biding the moon
Till dawn should clear that dim frontier, first seen
—The Chan's great continent. . . . Then faith, not fear
Nigh surged me witless. . . . Hearing the surf near—
I, wonder-breathing, kept the watch,—saw
The first palm chevron the first lighted hill.

And lowered. And they came out to us crying,
"The Great White Birds!" (O Madre Maria, still
One ship of these thou grantest safe returning;
Assure us through thy mantle's ageless blue!)
And record of more, floating in a casque,
Was tumbled from us under bare poles scudding;

47

And later hurricanes may claim more pawn. . . .
For here between two worlds, another, harsh,

This third, of water, tests the word; lo, here
Bewilderment and mutiny heap whelming
35 Laughter, and shadow cuts sleep from the heart
Almost as though the Moor's flung scimitar
Found more than flesh to fathom in its fall.
Yet under tempest-lash and surfeitings
Some inmost sob, half-heard, dissuades the abyss,
40 Merges the wind in measure to the waves,

Series on series, infinite,—till eyes
Starved wide on blackened tides, accrete—enclose
This turning rondure whole, this crescent ring
Sun-cusped and zoned with modulated fire
45 Like pearls that whisper through the Doge's hands
—Yet no delirium of jewels! O Fernando,
Take of that eastern shore, this western sea,
Yet yield thy God's, thy Virgin's charity!

—Rush down the plenitude, and you shall see
50 Isaiah counting famine on this lee!

   .   .   .

An herb, a stray branch among salty teeth,
The jellied weeds that drag the shore,—perhaps
Tomorrow's moon will grant us Saltes Bar—
Palos again,—a land cleared of long war.
55 Some Angelus environs the cordage tree;
Dark waters onward shake the dark prow free.

   .   .   .

O Thou who sleepest on Thyself, apart
Like ocean athwart lanes of death and birth,
And all the eddying breath between dost search
60   Cruelly with love thy parable of man,—
Inquisitor! incognizable Word
Of Eden and the enchained Sepulchre,
Into thy steep savannahs, burning blue,
Utter to loneliness the sail is true.

65   Who grindest oar, and arguing the mast
Subscribest holocaust of ships, O Thou
Within whose primal scan consummately
The glistening seignories of Ganges swim;—
Who sendest greeting by the corposant,
70   And Teneriffe's garnet—flamed it in a cloud,
Urging through night our passage to the Chan;—
Te Deum laudamus, for thy teeming span!

Of all that amplitude that time explores,
A needle in the sight, suspended north,—
75   Yielding by inference and discard, faith
And true appointment from the hidden shoal:
This disposition that thy night relates
From Moon to Saturn in one sapphire wheel:
The orbic wake of thy once whirling feet,
80   Elohim, still I hear thy sounding heel!

White toil of heaven's cordons, mustering
In holy rings all sails charged to the far
Hushed gleaming fields and pendant seething wheat
Of knowledge,—round thy brows unhooded now
85   —The kindled Crown! acceded of the poles
And biassed by full sails, meridians reel

Thy purpose—still one shore beyond desire!
The sea's green crying towers a-sway, Beyond

And kingdoms
90   naked in the
                                trembling heart—
            Te Deum laudamus
                            O Thou Hand of Fire

II
POWHATAN'S DAUGHTER

"—*Pocahuntus, a well-featured but wanton yong girle . . . of the age of eleven or twelve years, get the boyes forth with her into the market place, and make them wheele, falling on their hands, turning their heels upwards, whom she would followe, and wheele so herself, naked as she was, all the fort over.*"

THE HARBOR DAWN

Insistently through sleep—a tide of voices—
They meet you listening midway in your dream,
The long, tired sounds, fog-insulated noises:
Gongs in white surplices, beshrouded wails,
Far strum of fog horns . . . signals dispersed in veils.

And then a truck will lumber past the wharves
As winch engines begin throbbing on some deck;
Or a drunken stevedore's howl and thud below
Comes echoing alley-upward through dim snow.

And if they take your sleep away sometimes
They give it back again. Soft sleeves of sound
Attend the darkling harbor, the pillowed bay;
Somewhere out there in blankness steam

Spills into steam, and wanders, washed away
—Flurried by keen fifings, eddied
Among distant chiming buoys—adrift. The sky,

Cool feathery fold, suspends, distills
This wavering slumber. . . . Slowly—
Immemorially the window, the half-covered chair
Ask nothing but this sheath of pallid air.

And you beside me, blessèd now while sirens
Sing to us, stealthily weave us into day—
Serenely now, before day claims our eyes
Your cool arms murmurously about me lay.

While myriad snowy hands are clustering at the panes—

> your hands within my hands are deeds;
> my tongue upon your throat—singing

400 years and more . . . or is it from the soundless shore of sleep that time

recalls you to your love, there in a waking dream to merge your seed

53

arms close; eyes wide, undoubtful
                    dark
30   *drink the dawn—*
        a forest shudders in your hair!

                                                    —with whom?

The window goes blond slowly. Frostily clears.
From Cyclopean towers across Manhattan waters
—Two—three bright window-eyes aglitter, disk
35 The sun, released—aloft with cold gulls hither.

The fog leans one last moment on the sill.
Under the mistletoe of dreams, a star—
As though to join us at some distant hill—
Turns in the waking west and goes to sleep.

Who is the
woman with
us in the
dawn? . . .
whose is the
flesh our feet
have moved
upon?

VAN WINKLE

Macadam, gun-grey as the tunny's belt,
Leaps from Far Rockaway to Golden Gate:
Listen! the miles a hurdy-gurdy grinds—
Down gold arpeggios mile on mile unwinds.

Streets spread past store and factory—sped by sunlight and her smile . . .

5   Times earlier, when you hurried off to school,
—It is the same hour though a later day—
You walked with Pizarro in a copybook,
And Cortes rode up, reining tautly in—
Firmly as coffee grips the taste,—and away!

10   There was Priscilla's cheek close in the wind,
And Captain Smith, all beard and certainty,
And Rip Van Winkle bowing by the way,—
"Is this Sleepy Hollow, friend—?" And he—

Like Memory, she is time's truant, shall take you by the hand . . .

And Rip forgot the office hours,
15   *   and he forgot the pay;*
*   Van Winkle sweeps a tenement*
*   way down on Avenue A,—*

The grind-organ says . . . Remember, remember
The cinder pile at the end of the backyard
20   Where we stoned the family of young
Garter snakes under . . . And the monoplanes
We launched—with paper wings and twisted
Rubber bands . . . Recall—recall

                                    the rapid tongues
25   That flittered from under the ash heap day
After day whenever your stick discovered
Some sunning inch of unsuspecting fibre—
It flashed back at your thrust, as clean as fire.

And Rip was slowly made aware
30   *that he, Van Winkle, was not here*
      nor there. He woke and swore he'd seen Broadway
        a Catskill daisy chain in May—

So memory, that strikes a rhyme out of a box,
Or splits a random smell of flowers through glass—
35 Is it the whip stripped from the lilac tree
One day in spring my father took to me,
Or is it the Sabbatical, unconscious smile
My mother almost brought me once from church
And once only, as I recall—?

40 It flickered through the snow screen, blindly
It forsook her at the doorway, it was gone
Before I had left the window. It
Did not return with the kiss in the hall.

Macadam, gun-grey as the tunny's belt,
45 Leaps from Far Rockaway to Golden Gate. . . .
Keep hold of that nickel for car-change, Rip,—
Have you got your *"Times"*—?
And hurry along, Van Winkle—it's getting late!

THE RIVER

Stick your patent name on a signboard
brother—all over—going west—young man
Tintex—Japalac—Certain-teed Overalls ads
and lands sakes! under the new playbill ripped
*. . . and past
the din and
slogans of
the year—*
5 in the guaranteed corner—see Bert Williams what?
Minstrels when you steal a chicken just
save me the wing for if it isn't
Erie it ain't for miles around a
Mazda—and the telegraphic night coming on Thomas

10 a Ediford—and whistling down the tracks
a headlight rushing with the sound—can you
imagine—while an EXPRESS makes time like
SCIENCE—COMMERCE and the HOLYGHOST
15 RADIO ROARS IN EVERY HOME WE HAVE THE NORTHPOLE
WALLSTREET AND VIRGINBIRTH WITHOUT STONES OR
WIRES OR EVEN RUNning brooks connecting ears
and no more sermons windows flashing roar
breathtaking—as you like it . . . eh?

So the 20th Century—so
20 whizzed the Limited—roared by and left
three men, still hungry on the tracks, ploddingly
watching the tail lights wizen and converge, slip-
ping gimleted and neatly out of sight.

．　　　．　　　．　　　．　　　．　　　．　　　．

The last bear, shot drinking in the Dakotas
25 Loped under wires that span the mountain stream.
Keen instruments, strung to a vast precision
Bind town to town and dream to ticking dream.
But some men take their liquor slow—and count
—Though they'll confess no rosary nor clue—
*to those
whose
addresses*

57

30 The river's minute by the far brook's year.   *are never near*
  Under a world of whistles, wires and steam
  Caboose-like they go ruminating through
  Ohio, Indiana—blind baggage—
  To Cheyenne tagging . . . Maybe Kalamazoo.

35 Time's rendings, time's blendings they construe
  As final reckonings of fire and snow;
  Strange bird-wit, like the elemental gist
  Of unwalled winds they offer, singing low
  My Old Kentucky Home and *Casey Jones*,
40 *Some Sunny Day*. I heard a road-gang chanting so.
  And afterwards, who had a colt's eyes—one said,
  "Jesus! Oh I remember watermelon days!" And sped
  High in a cloud of merriment, recalled
45 "—And when my Aunt Sally Simpson smiled," he drawled—
  "It was almost Louisiana, long ago."
  "There's no place like Booneville though, Buddy,"
  One said, excising a last burr from his vest,
  "—For early trouting." Then peering in the can,
  "—But I kept on the tracks." Possessed, resigned,
50 He trod the fire down pensively and grinned,
  Spreading dry shingles of a beard. . . .

                         Behind
  My father's cannery works I used to see
  Rail-squatters ranged in nomad raillery,
55 The ancient men—wifeless or runaway
  Hobo-trekkers that forever search
  An empire wilderness of freight and rails.
  Each seemed a child, like me, on a loose perch,
  Holding to childhood like some termless play.
60 John, Jake or Charley, hopping the slow freight

—Memphis to Tallahassee—riding the rods,
Blind fists of nothing, humpty-dumpty clods.

Yet they touch something like a key perhaps.
From pole to pole across the hills, the states
65 —They know a body under the wide rain;
Youngsters with eyes like fjords, old reprobates
With racetrack jargon,—dotting immensity
They lurk across her, knowing her yonder breast
Snow-silvered, sumac-stained or smoky blue—
70 Is past the valley-sleepers, south or west.
—As I have trod the rumorous midnights, too,

*but who have
touched her,
knowing her
without name*

And past the circuit of the lamp's thin flame
(O Nights that brought me to her body bare!)
Have dreamed beyond the print that bound her name.
75 Trains sounding the long blizzards out—I heard
Wail into distances I knew were hers.
Papooses crying on the wind's long mane
Screamed redskin dynasties that fled the brain,
—Dead echoes! But I knew her body there,
80 Time like a serpent down her shoulder, dark,
And space, an eaglet's wing, laid on her hair.

Under the Ozarks, domed by Iron Mountain,
The old gods of the rain lie wrapped in pools
Where eyeless fish curvet a sunken fountain
85 And re-descend with corn from querulous crows.
Such pilferings make up their timeless eatage,
Propitiate them for their timber torn
By iron, iron—always the iron dealt cleavage!
They doze now, below axe and powder horn.

*nor the
myths of her
fathers . . .*

90 And Pullman breakfasters glide glistening steel
    From tunnel into field—iron strides the dew—
    Straddles the hill, a dance of wheel on wheel.
    You have a half-hour's wait at Siskiyou,
    Or stay the night and take the next train through.
95 Southward, near Cairo passing, you can see
    The Ohio merging,—borne down Tennessee;
    And if it's summer and the sun's in dusk
    Maybe the breeze will lift the River's musk
    —As though the waters breathed that you might know
100 *Memphis Johnny, Steamboat Bill, Missouri Joe.*
    Oh, lean from the window, if the train slows down,
    As though you touched hands with some ancient clown,
    —A little while gaze absently below
    And hum *Deep River* with them while they go.

105 Yes, turn again and sniff once more—look see,
    O Sheriff, Brakeman and Authority—
    Hitch up your pants and crunch another quid,
    For you, too, feed the River timelessly.
    And few evade full measure of their fate;
110 Always they smile out eerily what they seem.
    I could believe he joked at heaven's gate—
    Dan Midland—jolted from the cold brake-beam.

    Down, down—born pioneers in time's despite,
    Grimed tributaries to an ancient flow—
115 They win no frontier by their wayward plight,
    But drift in stillness, as from Jordan's brow.

    You will not hear it as the sea; even stone
    Is not more hushed by gravity . . . But slow,
    As loth to take more tribute—sliding prone
120 Like one whose eyes were buried long ago

The River, spreading, flows—and spends your dream.
What are you, lost within this tideless spell?
You are your father's father, and the stream—
A liquid theme that floating niggers swell.

125 Damp tonnage and alluvial march of days—
Nights turbid, vascular with silted shale
And roots surrendered down of moraine clays:
The Mississippi drinks the farthest dale.

O quarrying passion, undertowed sunlight!
130 The basalt surface drags a jungle grace
Ochreous and lynx-barred in lengthening might;
Patience! and you shall reach the biding place!

Over De Soto's bones the freighted floors
Throb past the City storied of three thrones.
135 Down two more turns the Mississippi pours
(Anon tall ironsides up from salt lagoons)

And flows within itself, heaps itself free.
All fades but one thin skyline 'round . . . Ahead
No embrace opens but the stinging sea;
140 The River lifts itself from its long bed,

Poised wholly on its dream, a mustard glow
Tortured with history, its one will—flow!
—The Passion spreads in wide tongues, choked and slow,
Meeting the Gulf, hosannas silently below.

THE DANCE

The swift red flesh, a winter king—
Who squired the glacier woman down the sky?
She ran the neighing canyons all the spring;
She spouted arms; she rose with maize—to die.

5 And in the autumn drouth, whose burnished hands
With mineral wariness found out the stone
Where prayers, forgotten, streamed the mesa sands?
He holds the twilight's dim, perpetual throne.

Mythical brows we saw retiring—loth,
10 Disturbed and destined, into denser green.
Greeting they sped us, on the arrow's oath:
Now lie incorrigibly what years between . . .

There was a bed of leaves, and broken play;
There was a veil upon you, Pocahontas, bride—
15 O Princess whose brown lap was virgin May;
And bridal flanks and eyes hid tawny pride.

I left the village for dogwood. By the canoe
Tugging below the mill-race, I could see
Your hair's keen crescent running, and the blue
20 First moth of evening take wing stealthily.

What laughing chains the water wove and threw!
I learned to catch the trout's moon whisper; I
Drifted how many hours I never knew,
But, watching, saw that fleet young crescent die,—

25 And one star, swinging, take its place, alone,
Cupped in the larches of the mountain pass—
Until, immortally, it bled into the dawn.
I left my sleek boat nibbling margin grass . . .

*Then you shall
see her truly
—your blood
remembering
its first
invasion of
her secrecy,
its first
encounters
with her kin,
her chieftain
lover . . . his
shade that
haunts the
lakes and hills*

I took the portage climb, then chose
30   A further valley-shed; I could not stop.
Feet nozzled wat'ry webs of upper flows;
One white veil gusted from the very top.

O Appalachian Spring! I gained the ledge;
Steep, inaccessible smile that eastward bends
35   And northward reaches in that violet wedge
Of Adirondacks!—wisped of azure wands,

Over how many bluffs, tarns, streams I sped!
—And knew myself within some boding shade:—
Grey tepees tufting the blue knolls ahead,
40   Smoke swirling through the yellow chestnut glade . . .

A distant cloud, a thunder-bud—it grew,
That blanket of the skies: the padded foot
Within,—I heard it; 'til its rhythm drew,
—Siphoned the black pool from the heart's hot root!

45   A cyclone threshes in the turbine crest,
Swooping in eagle feathers down your back;
Know, Maquokeeta, greeting; know death's best;
—Fall, Sachem, strictly as the tamarack!

A birch kneels. All her whistling fingers fly.
50   The oak grove circles in a crash of leaves;
The long moan of a dance is in the sky.
Dance, Maquokeeta: Pocahontas grieves . . .

And every tendon scurries toward the twangs
Of lightning deltaed down your saber hair.
55   Now snaps the flint in every tooth; red fangs
And splay tongues thinly busy the blue air . . .

Dance, Maquokeeta! snake that lives before,
That casts his pelt, and lives beyond! Sprout, horn!
Spark, tooth! Medicine-man, relent, restore—
60   Lie to us,—dance us back the tribal morn!

Spears and assemblies: black drums thrusting on—
O yelling battlements,—I, too, was liege
To rainbows currying each pulsant bone:
Surpassed the circumstance, danced out the siege!

65   And buzzard-circleted, screamed from the stake;
I could not pick the arrows from my side.
Wrapped in that fire, I saw more escorts wake—
Flickering, sprint up the hill groins like a tide.

I heard the hush of lava wrestling your arms,
70   And stag teeth foam about the raven throat;
Flame cataracts of heaven in seething swarms
Fed down your anklets to the sunset's moat.

O, like the lizard in the furious noon,
That drops his legs and colors in the sun,
75   —And laughs, pure serpent, Time itself, and moon
Of his own fate, I saw thy change begun!

And saw thee dive to kiss that destiny
Like one white meteor, sacrosanct and blent
At last with all that's consummate and free
80   There, where the first and last gods keep thy tent.

        ·   ·   ·   ·

Thewed of the levin, thunder-shod and lean,
Lo, through what infinite seasons dost thou gaze—

Across what bivouacs of thine angered slain,
And see'st thy bride immortal in the maize!

85   Totem and fire-gall, slumbering pyramid—
Though other calendars now stack the sky,
Thy freedom is her largesse, Prince, and hid
On paths thou knewest best to claim her by.

High unto Labrador the sun strikes free
90   Her speechless dream of snow, and stirred again,
She is the torrent and the singing tree;
And she is virgin to the last of men . . .

West, west and south! winds over Cumberland
And winds across the llano grass resume
95   Her hair's warm sibilance. Her breasts are fanned
O stream by slope and vineyard—into bloom!

And when the caribou slant down for salt
Do arrows thirst and leap? Do antlers shine
Alert, star-triggered in the listening vault
100   Of dusk?—And are her perfect brows to thine?

We danced, O Brave, we danced beyond their farms,
In cobalt desert closures made our vows . . .
Now is the strong prayer folded in thine arms,
The serpent with the eagle in the boughs.

INDIANA

The morning glory, climbing the morning long
    Over the lintel on its wiry vine,
Closes before the dusk, furls in its song
        As I close mine . . .

*. . . and read
her in a
mother's
farewell gaze.*

5   And bison thunder rends my dreams no more
    As once my womb was torn, my boy, when you
Yielded your first cry at the prairie's door . . .
        Your father knew

Then, though we'd buried him behind us, far
10   Back on the gold trail—then his lost bones stirred . . .
But you who drop the scythe to grasp the oar
        Knew not, nor heard

How we, too, Prodigal, once rode off, too—
    Waved Seminary Hill a gay good-bye . . .
15 We found God lavish there in Colorado
        But passing sly.

The pebbles sang, the firecat slunk away
    And glistening through the sluggard freshets came
In golden syllables loosed from the clay
20   His gleaming name.

A dream called Eldorado was his town,
    It rose up shambling in the nuggets' wake,
It had no charter but a promised crown
        Of claims to stake.

25 But we,—too late, too early, howsoever—
    Won nothing out of fifty-nine—those years—
But gilded promise, yielded to us never,
        And barren tears . . .

The long trail back! I huddled in the shade
   Of wagon-tenting looked out once and saw
30 Bent westward, passing on a stumbling jade
      A homeless squaw—

Perhaps a halfbreed. On her slender back
   She cradled a babe's body, riding without rein.
Her eyes, strange for an Indian's, were not black
35   But sharp with pain

And like twin stars. They seemed to shun the gaze
   Of all our silent men—the long team line—
Until she saw me—when their violet haze
      Lit with love shine . . .

40 I held you up—I suddenly the bolder,
   Knew that mere words could not have brought us nearer.
She nodded—and that smile across her shoulder
      Will still endear her

As long as Jim, your father's memory, is warm.
45   Yes, Larry, now you're going to sea, remember
You were the first—before Ned and this farm,—
      First-born, remember—

And since then—all that's left to me of Jim
   Whose folks, like mine, came out of Arrowhead.
50 And you're the only one with eyes like him—
      Kentucky bred!

I'm standing still, I'm old, I'm half of stone!
   Oh, hold me in those eyes' engaging blue;
There's where the stubborn years gleam and atone,—
55   Where gold is true!

Down the dim turnpike to the river's edge—
    Perhaps I'll hear the mare's hoofs to the ford . . .
Write me from Rio . . . and you'll keep your pledge;
      I know your word!

60 Come back to Indiana—not too late!
    (Or will you be a ranger to the end?)
Good-bye . . . Good-bye . . . oh, I shall always wait
    You, Larry, traveller—
                stranger,
65   son,
                          —my friend—

III
CUTTY SARK

O, the navies old and oaken,
O, the Temeraire no more!
—MELVILLE

CUTTY SARK

I met a man in South Street, tall—
a nervous shark tooth swung on his chain.
His eyes pressed through green glass
—green glasses, or bar lights made them
5   so—
        shine—
                GREEN—
                        eyes—
stepped out—forgot to look at you
10 or left you several blocks away—

in the nickel-in-the-slot piano jogged
"Stamboul Nights"—weaving somebody's nickel—sang—

    O Stamboul Rose—dreams weave the rose!

        Murmurs of Leviathan he spoke,
15   and rum was Plato in our heads . . .

"It's *S.S. Ala*—Antwerp—now remember kid
to put me out at three she sails on time.
I'm not much good at time any more keep
weakeyed watches sometimes snooze—" his bony hands
20 got to beating time . . . "A whaler once—
I ought to keep time and get over it—I'm a
Democrat—I know what time it is—No
I don't want to know what time it is—that
damned white Arctic killed my time . . ."

25   *O Stamboul Rose—drums weave—*

"I ran a donkey engine down there on the Canal
in Panama—got tired of that—
then Yucatan selling kitchenware—beads—

have you seen Popocatepetl—birdless mouth
30   with ashes sifting down—?
                                        and then the coast again . . ."

        Rose of Stamboul O coral Queen—
        teased remnants of the skeletons of cities—
        and galleries, galleries of watergutted lava
35   *snarling stone—green—drums—drown—*

Sing!
"—that spiracle!" he shot a finger out the door . . .
"O life's a geyser—beautiful—my lungs—
No—I can't live on land—!"

40   I saw the frontiers gleaming of his mind;
or are there frontiers—running sands sometimes
running sands—somewhere—sands running . . .
Or they may start some white machine that sings.
Then you may laugh and dance the axletree—
45   steel—silver—kick the traces—and know—

        ATLANTIS ROSE drums wreathe the rose,
        the star floats burning in a gulf of tears
        and sleep another thousand—

                                        interminably
50   long since somebody's nickel—stopped—
playing—

A wind worried those wicker-neat lapels, the
swinging summer entrances to cooler hells . . .
Outside a wharf truck nearly ran him down
55   —he lunged up Bowery way while the dawn

was putting the Statue of Liberty out—that
torch of hers you know—

I started walking home across the Bridge . . .

    •   •   •   •   •

Blithe Yankee vanities, turreted sprites, winged
60   British repartees, skil-
ful savage sea-girls
that bloomed in the spring—Heave, weave
those bright designs the trade winds drive . . .

    Sweet opium and tea, Yo-ho!
65   *Pennies for porpoises that bank the keel!*
    Fins whip the breeze around Japan!

Bright skysails ticketing the Line, wink round the Horn
to Frisco, Melbourne . . .
                            Pennants, parabolas—
70 clipper dreams indelible and ranging,
baronial white on lucky blue!

    Perennial-*Cutty*-trophied-*Sark*!

Thermopylae, Black Prince, Flying Cloud through Sunda
—scarfed of foam, their bellies veered green esplanades,
75 locked in wind-humors, ran their eastings down;

    at Java Head freshened the nip
    (sweet opium and tea!)
    and turned and left us on the lee . . .

Buntlines tusseling (91 days, 20 hours and anchored!)
80   *Rainbow, Leander*

(last trip a tragedy)—where can you be
Nimbus? and you rivals two—

      a long tack keeping—

                                  Taeping?

85   *Ariel*?

IV
CAPE HATTERAS

The seas all crossed,
weathered the capes, the voyage done . . .
—WALT WHITMAN

CAPE HATTERAS

Imponderable the dinosaur
                sinks slow,
                       the mammoth saurian
                             ghoul, the eastern
5   Cape . . .
While rises in the west the coastwise range,
                       slowly the hushed land—
Combustion at the astral core—the dorsal change
Of energy—convulsive shift of sand . . .
10 But we, who round the capes, the promontories
Where strange tongues vary messages of surf
Below grey citadels, repeating to the stars
The ancient names—return home to our own
Hearths, there to eat an apple and recall
15 The songs that gypsies dealt us at Marseille
Or how the priests walked—slowly through Bombay—
Or to read you, Walt,—knowing us in thrall

To that deep wonderment, our native clay
Whose depth of red, eternal flesh of Pocahontas—
20 Those continental folded aeons, surcharged
With sweetness below derricks, chimneys, tunnels—
Is veined by all that time has really pledged us . . .
And from above, thin squeaks of radio static,
The captured fume of space foams in our ears—
25 What whisperings of far watches on the main
Relapsing into silence, while time clears
Our lenses, lifts a focus, resurrects
A periscope to glimpse what joys or pain
Our eyes can share or answer—then deflects
30 Us, shunting to a labyrinth submersed
Where each sees only his dim past reversed . . .

But that star-glistered salver of infinity,
The circle, blind crucible of endless space,

Is sluiced by motion,—subjugated never.
35   Adam and Adam's answer in the forest
Left Hesperus mirrored in the lucid pool.
Now the eagle dominates our days, is jurist
Of the ambiguous cloud. We know the strident rule
Of wings imperious . . . Space, instantaneous,
40   Flickers a moment, consumes us in its smile:
A flash over the horizon—shifting gears—
And we have laughter, or more sudden tears.
Dream cancels dream in this new realm of fact
From which we wake into the dream of act;
45   Seeing himself an atom in a shroud—
Man hears himself an engine in a cloud!

"—Recorders ages hence"—ah, syllables of faith!
Walt, tell me, Walt Whitman, if infinity
Be still the same as when you walked the beach
50   Near Paumanok—your lone patrol—and heard the wraith
Through surf, its bird note there a long time falling . . .
For you, the panoramas and this breed of towers,
Of you—the theme that's statured in the cliff,
O Saunterer on free ways still ahead!
55   Not this our empire yet, but labyrinth
Wherein your eyes, like the Great Navigator's without ship,
Gleam from the great stones of each prison crypt
Of canyoned traffic . . . Confronting the Exchange,
Surviving in a world of stocks,—they also range
60   Across the hills where second timber strays
Back over Connecticut farms, abandoned pastures,—
Sea eyes and tidal, undenying, bright with myth!

The nasal whine of power whips a new universe . . .
Where spouting pillars spoor the evening sky,
65   Under the looming stacks of the gigantic power house

Stars prick the eyes with sharp ammoniac proverbs,
New verities, new inklings in the velvet hummed
Of dynamos, where hearing's leash is strummed . . .
Power's script,—wound, bobbin-bound, refined—
70 Is stropped to the slap of belts on booming spools, spurred
Into the bulging bouillon, harnessed jelly of the stars.
Towards what? The forked crash of split thunder parts
Our hearing momentwise; but fast in whirling armatures,
As bright as frogs' eyes, giggling in the girth
75 Of steely gizzards—axle-bound, confined
In coiled precision, bunched in mutual glee
The bearings glint,—O murmurless and shined
In oilrinsed circles of blind ecstasy!

Stars scribble on our eyes the frosty sagas,
80 The gleaming cantos of unvanquished space . . .
O sinewy silver biplane, nudging the wind's withers!
There, from Kill Devils Hill at Kitty Hawk
Two brothers in their twinship left the dune;
Warping the gale, the Wright windwrestlers veered
85 Capeward, then blading the wind's flank, banked and spun
What ciphers risen from prophetic script,
What marathons new-set between the stars!
The soul, by naphtha fledged into new reaches
Already knows the closer clasp of Mars,—
90 New latitudes, unknotting, soon give place
To what fierce schedules, rife of doom apace!

Behold the dragon's covey—amphibian, ubiquitous
To hedge the seaboard, wrap the headland, ride
The blue's cloud-templed districts unto ether . . .
95 While Iliads glimmer through eyes raised in pride
Hell's belt springs wider into heaven's plumed side.
O bright circumferences, heights employed to fly

War's fiery kennel masked in downy offings,—
This tournament of space, the threshed and chiselled height,
100 Is baited by marauding circles, bludgeon flail
Of rancorous grenades whose screaming petals carve us
Wounds that we wrap with theorems sharp as hail!

Wheeled swiftly, wings emerge from larval-silver hangars.
Taut motors surge, space-gnawing, into flight;
105 Through sparkling visibility, outspread, unsleeping,
Wings clip the last peripheries of light . . .
Tellurian wind-sleuths on dawn patrol,
Each plane a hurtling javelin of winged ordnance,
Bristle the heights above a screeching gale to hover;
110 Surely no eye that Sunward Escadrille can cover!
There, meaningful, fledged as the Pleiades
With razor sheen they zoom each rapid helix!
Up-chartered choristers of their own speeding
They, cavalcade on escapade, shear Cumulus—
115 Lay siege and hurdle Cirrus down the skies!
While Cetus-like, O thou Dirigible, enormous Lounger
Of pendulous auroral beaches,—satellited wide
By convoy planes, moonferrets that rejoin thee
On fleeing balconies as thou dost glide,
120 —Hast splintered space!

Low, shadowed of the Cape,
Regard the moving turrets! From grey decks
See scouting griffons rise through gaseous crepe
Hung low . . . until a conch of thunder answers
125 Cloud-belfries, banging, while searchlights, like fencers,
Slit the sky's pancreas of foaming anthracite
Toward thee, O Corsair of the typhoon,—pilot, hear!
Thine eyes bicarbonated white by speed, O Skygak, see
How from thy path above the levin's lance

130 Thou sowest doom thou hast nor time nor chance
To reckon—as thy stilly eyes partake
What alcohol of space . . ! Remember, Falcon-Ace,
Thou hast there in thy wrist a Sanskrit charge
To conjugate infinity's dim marge—
135 Anew . . !

              But first, here at this height receive
The benediction of the shell's deep, sure reprieve!
Lead-perforated fuselage, escutcheoned wings
Lift agonized quittance, tilting from the invisible brink
140 Now eagle-bright, now
                      quarry-hid, twist-
                               -ing, sink with
Enormous repercussive list-
                    -ings down
145 Giddily spiralled
                gauntlets, upturned, unlooping
In guerrilla sleights, trapped in combustion gyr-
Ing, dance the curdled depth
                      down whizzing
150 Zodiacs, dashed
             (now nearing fast the Cape!)
                     down gravitation's
                         vortex into crashed
. . . . dispersion . . . into mashed and shapeless debris. . . .
155 By Hatteras bunched the beached heap of high bravery!

       •   •   •   •   •   •

The stars have grooved our eyes with old persuasions
Of love and hatred, birth,—surcease of nations . . .
But who has held the heights more sure than thou,
O Walt!—Ascensions of thee hover in me now

160   As thou at junctions elegiac, there, of speed
       With vast eternity, dost wield the rebound seed!
       The competent loam, the probable grass,—travail
       Of tides awash the pedestal of Everest, fail
       Not less than thou in pure impulse inbred
165   To answer deepest soundings! O, upward from the dead
       Thou bringest tally, and a pact, new bound
       Of living brotherhood!

                    Thou, there beyond—
       Glacial sierras and the flight of ravens,
170   Hermetically past condor zones, through zenith havens
       Past where the albatross has offered up
       His last wing-pulse, and downcast as a cup
       That's drained, is shivered back to earth—thy wand
       Has beat a song, O Walt,—there and beyond!
175   And this, thine other hand, upon my heart
       Is plummet ushered of those tears that start
       What memories of vigils, bloody, by that Cape,—
       Ghoul-mound of man's perversity at balk
       And fraternal massacre! Thou, pallid there as chalk
180   Hast kept of wounds, O Mourner, all that sum
       That then from Appomattox stretched to Somme!

       Cowslip and shad-blow, flaked like tethered foam
       Around bared teeth of stallions, bloomed that spring
       When first I read thy lines, rife as the loam
185   Of prairies, yet like breakers cliffward leaping!
       O, early following thee, I searched the hill
       Blue-writ and odor-firm with violets, 'til
       With June the mountain laurel broke through green
       And filled the forest with what clustrous sheen!
190   Potomac lilies,—then the Pontiac rose,
       And Klondike edelweiss of occult snows!

White banks of moonlight came descending valleys—
How speechful on oak-vizored palisades,
As vibrantly I following down Sequoia alleys
95   Heard thunder's eloquence through green arcades
Set trumpets breathing in each clump and grass tuft—'til
Gold autumn, captured, crowned the trembling hill!

Panis Angelicus! Eyes tranquil with the blaze
Of love's own diametric gaze, of love's amaze!
00   Not greatest, thou,—not first, nor last,—but near
And onward yielding past my utmost year.
Familiar, thou, as mendicants in public places;
Evasive—too—as dayspring's spreading arc to trace is:—
Our Meistersinger, thou set breath in steel;
05   And it was thou who on the boldest heel
Stood up and flung the span on even wing
Of that great Bridge, our Myth, whereof I sing!

Years of the Modern! Propulsions toward what capes?
But thou, *Panis Angelicus*, hast thou not seen
10   And passed that Barrier that none escapes—
But knows it leastwise as death-strife?—O, something green,
Beyond all sesames of science was thy choice
Wherewith to bind us throbbing with one voice,
New integers of Roman, Viking, Celt—
15   Thou, Vedic Caesar, to the greensward knelt!

And now, as launched in abysmal cupolas of space,
Toward endless terminals, Easters of speeding light—
Vast engines outward veering with seraphic grace
On clarion cylinders pass out of sight
20   To course that span of consciousness thou'st named
The Open Road—thy vision is reclaimed!
What heritage thou'st signalled to our hands!

And see! the rainbow's arch—how shimmeringly stands
Above the Cape's ghoul-mound, O joyous seer!
225   Recorders ages hence, yes, they shall hear
In their own veins uncancelled thy sure tread
And read thee by the aureole 'round thy head
Of pasture-shine, *Panis Angelicus*!

                                yes, Walt,
230   Afoot again, and onward without halt,—
Not soon, nor suddenly,—no, never to let go
    My hand
         in yours,
              Walt Whitman—
235   so—

V
THREE SONGS

The one Sestos, the other Abydos hight.
—MARLOWE

SOUTHERN CROSS

I wanted you, nameless Woman of the South,
No wraith, but utterly—as still more alone
The Southern Cross takes night
And lifts her girdles from her, one by one—
High, cool,
                    wide from the slowly smoldering fire
Of lower heavens,—
                    vaporous scars!

Eve! Magdalene!
                    or Mary, you?

Whatever call—falls vainly on the wave.
O simian Venus, homeless Eve,
Unwedded, stumbling gardenless to grieve
Windswept guitars on lonely decks forever;
Finally to answer all within one grave!

And this long wake of phosphor,
                                        iridescent
Furrow of all our travel—trailed derision!
Eyes crumble at its kiss. Its long-drawn spell
Incites a yell. Slid on that backward vision
The mind is churned to spittle, whispering hell.

I wanted you . . . The embers of the Cross
Climbed by aslant and huddling aromatically.
It is blood to remember; it is fire
To stammer back . . . It is
God—your namelessness. And the wash—

All night the water combed you with black
Insolence. You crept out simmering, accomplished.
Water rattled that stinging coil, your

30 Rehearsed hair—docile, alas, from many arms.
Yes, Eve—wraith of my unloved seed!

The Cross, a phantom, buckled—dropped below the dawn.
Light drowned the lithic trillions of your spawn.

NATIONAL WINTER GARDEN

Outspoken buttocks in pink beads
Invite the necessary cloudy clinch
Of bandy eyes. . . . No extra mufflings here:
The world's one flagrant, sweating cinch.

And while legs waken salads in the brain
You pick your blonde out neatly through the smoke.
Always you wait for someone else though, always—
(Then rush the nearest exit through the smoke).

Always and last, before the final ring
When all the fireworks blare, begins
A tom-tom scrimmage with a somewhere violin,
Some cheapest echo of them all—begins.

And shall we call her whiter than the snow?
Sprayed first with ruby, then with emerald sheen—
Least tearful and least glad (who knows her smile?)
A caught slide shows her sandstone grey between.

Her eyes exist in swivellings of her teats,
Pearls whip her hips, a drench of whirling strands.
Her silly snake rings begin to mount, surmount
Each other—turquoise fakes on tinselled hands.

We wait that writhing pool, her pearls collapsed,
—All but her belly buried in the floor;
And the lewd trounce of a final muted beat!
We flee her spasm through a fleshless door. . . .

Yet, to the empty trapeze of your flesh,
O Magdalene, each comes back to die alone.
Then you, the burlesque of our lust—and faith,
Lug us back lifeward—bone by infant bone.

89

VIRGINIA

O rain at seven,
Pay-check at eleven—
Keep smiling the boss away,
Mary (what are you going to do?)
Gone seven—gone eleven,
And I'm still waiting you—

O blue-eyed Mary with the claret scarf,
Saturday Mary, mine!

It's high carillon
From the popcorn bells!
Pigeons by the million—
And Spring in Prince Street
Where green figs gleam
By oyster shells!

O Mary, leaning from the high wheat tower,
Let down your golden hair!

High in the noon of May
On cornices of daffodils
The slender violets stray.
Crap-shooting gangs in Bleecker reign,
Peonies with pony manes—
Forget-me-nots at windowpanes:

Out of the way-up nickel-dime tower shine,
Cathedral Mary,
                                    shine!—

VI
QUAKER HILL

*I see only the ideal. But no ideals
have ever been fully successful on
this earth.*
 —ISADORA DUNCAN

*The gentian weaves her fringes,
The maple's loom is red.*
 —EMILY DICKINSON

QUAKER HILL

Perspective never withers from their eyes;
They keep that docile edict of the Spring
That blends March with August Antarctic skies:
These are but cows that see no other thing
Than grass and snow, and their own inner being
Through the rich halo that they do not trouble
Even to cast upon the seasons fleeting
Though they should thin and die on last year's stubble.

And they are awkward, ponderous and uncoy . . .
While we who press the cider mill, regarding them—
We, who with pledges taste the bright annoy
Of friendship's acid wine, retarding phlegm,
Shifting reprisals ('til who shall tell us when
The jest is too sharp to be kindly?) boast
Much of our store of faith in other men
Who would, ourselves, stalk down the merriest ghost.

Above them old Mizzentop, palatial white
Hostelry—floor by floor to cinquefoil dormer
Portholes the ceilings stack their stoic height.
Long tiers of windows staring out toward former
Faces—loose panes crown the hill and gleam
At sunset with a silent, cobwebbed patience . . .
See them, like eyes that still uphold some dream
Through mapled vistas, cancelled reservations!

High from the central cupola, they say
One's glance could cross the borders of three states;
But I have seen death's stare in slow survey
From four horizons that no one relates . . .
Weekenders avid of their turf-won scores,
Here three hours from the semaphores, the Czars

Of golf, by twos and threes in plaid plusfours
Alight with sticks abristle and cigars.

This was the Promised Land, and still it is
To the persuasive suburban land agent
35   In bootleg roadhouses where the gin fizz
Bubbles in time to Hollywood's new love-nest pageant.
Fresh from the radio in the old Meeting House
(Now the New Avalon Hotel) volcanoes roar
A welcome to highsteppers that no mouse
40   Who saw the Friends there ever heard before.

What cunning neighbors history has in fine!
The woodlouse mortgages the ancient deal
Table that Powitzky buys for only nine-
Ty-five at Adams' auction,—eats the seal,
45   The spinster polish of antiquity . . .
Who holds the lease on time and on disgrace?
What eats the pattern with ubiquity?
Where are my kinsmen and the patriarch race?

The resigned factions of the dead preside.
50   Dead rangers bled their comfort on the snow;
But I must ask slain Iroquois to guide
Me farther than scalped Yankees knew to go:
Shoulder the curse of sundered parentage,
Wait for the postman driving from Birch Hill
55   With birthright by blackmail, the arrant page
That unfolds a new destiny to fill. . . .

So, must we from the hawk's far stemming view,
Must we descend as worm's eye to construe
Our love of all we touch, and take it to the Gate

60 As humbly as a guest who knows himself too late,
    His news already told? Yes, while the heart is wrung,
    Arise—yes, take this sheaf of dust upon your tongue!
    In one last angelus lift throbbing throat—
    Listen, transmuting silence with that stilly note

65 Of pain that Emily, that Isadora knew!
    While high from dim elm-chancels hung with dew,
    That triple-noted clause of moonlight—
    Yes, whip-poor-will, unhusks the heart of fright,
    Breaks us and saves, yes, breaks the heart, yet yields
70 That patience that is armour and that shields
    Love from despair—when love foresees the end—
    Leaf after autumnal leaf
                            break off,
                                    descend—
75   descend—

VII
THE TUNNEL

To Find the Western path
Right thro' the Gates of Wrath.
—BLAKE

THE TUNNEL

Performances, assortments, résumés—
Up Times Square to Columbus Circle lights
Channel the congresses, nightly sessions,
Refractions of the thousand theatres, faces—
5   Mysterious kitchens. . . . You shall search them all.
Someday by heart you'll learn each famous sight
And watch the curtain lift in hell's despite;
You'll find the garden in the third act dead,
Finger your knees—and wish yourself in bed
10 With tabloid crime-sheets perched in easy sight.

      Then let you reach your hat
      and go.
      As usual, let you—also
      walking down—exclaim
15   to twelve upward leaving
      a subscription praise
      for what time slays.

Or can't you quite make up your mind to ride;
A walk is better underneath the L a brisk
20 Ten blocks or so before? But you find yourself
Preparing penguin flexions of the arms,—
As usual you will meet the scuttle yawn:
The subway yawns the quickest promise home.

Be minimum, then, to swim the hiving swarms
25 Out of the Square, the Circle burning bright—
Avoid the glass doors gyring at your right,
Where boxed alone a second, eyes take fright
—Quite unprepared rush naked back to light:
And down beside the turnstile press the coin
30 Into the slot. The gongs already rattle.

And so
of cities you bespeak
subways, rivered under streets
and rivers. . . . In the car
35   the overtone of motion
underground, the monotone
of motion is the sound
of other faces, also underground—

"Let's have a pencil Jimmy—living now
40   at Floral Park
Flatbush—on the fourth of July—
like a pigeon's muddy dream—potatoes
to dig in the field—travlin the town—too—
night after night—the Culver line—the
45   girls all shaping up—it used to be—"

Our tongues recant like beaten weather vanes.
This answer lives like verdigris, like hair
Beyond extinction, surcease of the bone;
And repetition freezes—"What

50   "what do you want? getting weak on the links?
fandaddle daddy don't ask for change—IS THIS
FOURTEENTH? it's half past six she said—if
you don't like my gate why did you
swing on it, why *didja*
55   swing on it
anyhow—"

And somehow anyhow swing—

The phonographs of hades in the brain
Are tunnels that re-wind themselves, and love

60   A burnt match skating in a urinal—
Somewhere above Fourteenth TAKE THE EXPRESS
To brush some new presentiment of pain—

"But I want service in this office SERVICE
I said—after
65   the show she cried a little afterwards but—"

Whose head is swinging from the swollen strap?
Whose body smokes along the bitten rails,
Bursts from a smoldering bundle far behind
In back forks of the chasms of the brain,—
70   Puffs from a riven stump far out behind
In interborough fissures of the mind . . . ?

And why do I often meet your visage here,
Your eyes like agate lanterns—on and on
Below the toothpaste and the dandruff ads?
75   —And did their riding eyes right through your side,
And did their eyes like unwashed platters ride?
And Death, aloft,—gigantically down
Probing through you—toward me, O evermore!
And when they dragged your retching flesh,
80   Your trembling hands that night through Baltimore—
That last night on the ballot rounds, did you,
Shaking, did you deny the ticket, Poe?

For Gravesend Manor change at Chambers Street.
The platform hurries along to a dead stop.

85   The intent escalator lifts a serenade
Stilly
Of shoes, umbrellas, each eye attending its shoe, then
Bolting outright somewhere above where streets

Burst suddenly in rain. . . . The gongs recur:
90 Elbows and levers, guard and hissing door.
Thunder is galvothermic here below. . . . The car
Wheels off. The train rounds, bending to a scream,
Taking the final level for the dive
Under the river—
95 And somewhat emptier than before,
Demented, for a hitching second, humps; then
Lets go. . . . Toward corners of the floor
Newspapers wing, revolve and wing.
Blank windows gargle signals through the roar.

100 And does the Daemon take you home, also,
Wop washerwoman, with the bandaged hair?
After the corridors are swept, the cuspidors—
The gaunt sky-barracks cleanly now, and bare,
O Genoese, do you bring mother eyes and hands
105 Back home to children and to golden hair?

Daemon, demurring and eventful yawn!
Whose hideous laughter is a bellows mirth
—Or the muffled slaughter of a day in birth—
O cruelly to inoculate the brinking dawn
110 With antennae toward worlds that glow and sink;—
To spoon us out more liquid than the dim
Locution of the eldest star, and pack
The conscience navelled in the plunging wind,
Umbilical to call—and straightway die!

115 O caught like pennies beneath soot and steam,
Kiss of our agony thou gatherest;
Condensed, thou takest all—shrill ganglia
Impassioned with some song we fail to keep.
And yet, like Lazarus, to feel the slope,

120   The sod and billow breaking,—lifting ground,
     —A sound of waters bending astride the sky
     Unceasing with some Word that will not die . . . !

         •   •   •   •   •

     A tugboat, wheezing wreaths of steam,
     Lunged past, with one galvanic blare stove up the River.
125   I counted the echoes assembling, one after one,
     Searching, thumbing the midnight on the piers.
     Lights, coasting, left the oily tympanum of waters;
     The blackness somewhere gouged glass on a sky.
     And this thy harbor, O my City, I have driven under,
130   Tossed from the coil of ticking towers. . . . Tomorrow,
     And to be. . . . Here by the River that is East—
     Here at the waters' edge the hands drop memory;
     Shadowless in that abyss they unaccounting lie.
     How far away the star has pooled the sea—
135   Or shall the hands be drawn away, to die?

     Kiss of our agony Thou gatherest,
                   O Hand of Fire
                         gatherest—

VIII
ATLANTIS

*Music is then the knowledge of that which
relates to love in harmony and system.*
—PLATO

ATLANTIS

Through the bound cable strands, the arching path
Upward, veering with light, the flight of strings,—
Taut miles of shuttling moonlight syncopate
The whispered rush, telepathy of wires.
5   Up the index of night, granite and steel—
Transparent meshes—fleckless the gleaming staves—
Sibylline voices flicker, waveringly stream
As though a god were issue of the strings. . . .

And through that cordage, threading with its call
10   One arc synoptic of all tides below—
Their labyrinthine mouths of history
Pouring reply as though all ships at sea
Complighted in one vibrant breath made cry,—
"Make thy love sure—to weave whose song we ply!"
15   —From black embankments, moveless soundings hailed,
So seven oceans answer from their dream.

And on, obliquely up bright carrier bars
New octaves trestle the twin monoliths
Beyond whose frosted capes the moon bequeaths
20   Two worlds of sleep (O arching strands of song!)—
Onward and up the crystal-flooded aisle
White tempest nets file upward, upward ring
With silver terraces the humming spars,
The loft of vision, palladium helm of stars.

25   Sheerly the eyes, like seagulls stung with rime—
Slit and propelled by glistening fins of light—
Pick biting way up towering looms that press
Sidelong with flight of blade on tendon blade
—Tomorrows into yesteryear—and link
30   What cipher-script of time no traveller reads

But who, through smoking pyres of love and death,
Searches the timeless laugh of mythic spears.

Like hails, farewells—up planet-sequined heights
Some trillion whispering hammers glimmer Tyre:
35 Serenely, sharply up the long anvil cry
Of inchling aeons silence rivets Troy.
And you, aloft there—Jason! hesting Shout!
Still wrapping harness to the swarming air!
Silvery the rushing wake, surpassing call,
40 Beams yelling Aeolus! splintered in the straits!

From gulfs unfolding, terrible of drums,
Tall Vision-of-the-Voyage, tensely spare—
Bridge, lifting night to cycloramic crest
Of deepest day—O Choir, translating time
45 Into what multitudinous Verb the suns
And synergy of waters ever fuse, recast
In myriad syllables,—Psalm of Cathay!
O Love, thy white, pervasive Paradigm . . . !

We left the haven hanging in the night—
50 Sheened harbor lanterns backward fled the keel.
Pacific here at time's end, bearing corn,—
Eyes stammer through the pangs of dust and steel.
And still the circular, indubitable frieze
Of heaven's meditation, yoking wave
55 To kneeling wave, one song devoutly binds—
The vernal strophe chimes from deathless strings!

O Thou steeled Cognizance whose leap commits
The agile precincts of the lark's return;
Within whose lariat sweep encinctured sing
60 In single chrysalis the many twain,—

Of stars Thou art the stitch and stallion glow
And like an organ, Thou, with sound of doom—
Sight, sound and flesh Thou leadest from time's realm
As love strikes clear direction for the helm.

65 Swift peal of secular light, intrinsic Myth
Whose fell unshadow is death's utter wound,—
O River-throated—iridescently upborne
Through the bright drench and fabric of our veins;
With white escarpments swinging into light,
70 Sustained in tears the cities are endowed
And justified conclamant with ripe fields
Revolving through their harvests in sweet torment.

Forever Deity's glittering Pledge, O Thou
Whose canticle fresh chemistry assigns
75 To wrapt inception and beatitude,—
Always through blinding cables, to our joy,
Of thy white seizure springs the prophecy:
Always through spiring cordage, pyramids
Of silver sequel, Deity's young name
80 Kinetic of white choiring wings . . . ascends.

Migrations that must needs void memory,
Inventions that cobblestone the heart,—
Unspeakable Thou Bridge to Thee, O Love.
Thy pardon for this history, whitest Flower,
85 O Answerer of all,—Anemone,—
Now while thy petals spend the suns about us, hold—
(O Thou whose radiance doth inherit me)
Atlantis,—hold thy floating singer late!

So to thine Everpresence, beyond time,
90 Like spears ensanguined of one tolling star

That bleeds infinity—the orphic strings,
Sidereal phalanxes, leap and converge:
—One Song, one Bridge of Fire! Is it Cathay,
Now pity steeps the grass and rainbows ring
95 The serpent with the eagle in the leaves . . . ?
Whispers antiphonal in azure swing.

KEY WEST

An Island Sheaf

The starry floor,
The wat'ry shore,
Is given thee 'til the break of day.
　　　　　　　—BLAKE

O CARIB ISLE!

The tarantula rattling at the lily's foot
Across the feet of the dead, laid in white sand
Near the coral beach—nor zigzag fiddle crabs
Side-stilting from the path (that shift, subvert
And anagrammatize your name)—No, nothing here
Below the palsy that one eucalyptus lifts
In wrinkled shadows—mourns.

                    And yet suppose
I count these nacreous frames of tropic death,
Brutal necklaces of shells around each grave
Squared off so carefully. Then

To the white sand I may speak a name, fertile
Albeit in a stranger tongue. Tree names, flower names
Deliberate, gainsay death's brittle crypt. Meanwhile
The wind that knots itself in one great death—
Coils and withdraws. So syllables want breath.

But where is the Captain of this doubloon isle
Without a turnstile? Who but catchword crabs
Patrols the dry groins of the underbrush?
What man, or What
Is Commissioner of mildew throughout the ambushed senses?
His Carib mathematics web the eyes' baked lenses!

Under the poinciana, of a noon or afternoon
Let fiery blossoms clot the light, render my ghost
Sieved upward, white and black along the air
Until it meets the blue's comedian host.

Let not the pilgrim see himself again
For slow evisceration bound like those huge terrapin
Each daybreak on the wharf, their brine caked eyes;

30   —Spiked, overturned; such thunder in their strain!
       And clenched beaks coughing for the surge again!

       Slagged of the hurricane—I, cast within its flow,
       Congeal by afternoons here, satin and vacant.
       You have given me the shell, Satan,—carbonic amulet
35   Sere of the sun exploded in the sea.

THE MERMEN

And if
Thy banished trunk be found in our dominions—
KING LEAR

Buddhas and engines serve us undersea;
Though why they bide here, only hell that's sacked
Of every blight and ingenuity—
Can solve.

5   The Cross alone has flown the wave.
But since the Cross sank, much that's warped and cracked
Has followed in its name, has heaped its grave.
                          Oh—

Gallows and guillotines to hail the sun
10 And smoking wracks for penance when day's done!
                           No—

Leave us, you idols of Futurity—alone,
Here where we finger moidores of spent grace
And ponder the bright stains that starred this Throne

15 —This Cross, agleam still with a human Face!

113

TO
THE CLOUD JUGGLER

In Memoriam: Harry Crosby

What you may cluster 'round the knees of space
We hold in vision only, asking trace
Of districts where cliff, sea and palm advance
The falling wonder of a rainbow's trance.

5   Your light lifts whiteness into virgin azure . . .
Disclose your lips, O Sun, nor long demure
With snore of thunder, crowding us to bleed
The green preëmption of the deep seaweed.

You, the rum-giver to that slide-by-night,—
10   The moon's best lover,—guide us by a sleight
Of quarts to faithfuls—surely smuggled home—
As you raise temples fresh from basking foam.

Expose vaunted validities that yawn
Past pleasantries . . . Assert the ripened dawn
15   As you have yielded balcony and room
Or tempests—in a silver, floating plume.

Wrap us and lift us; drop us then, returned
Like water, undestroyed,—like mist, unburned . . .
But do not claim a friend like him again,
20   Whose arrow must have pierced you beyond pain.

THE MANGO TREE

Let them return, saying you blush again for the great
Great-grandmother. It's all like Christmas.
When you sprouted Paradise a discard of chewing-gum
took place. Up jug to musical, hanging jug just gay spiders
yoked you first,—silking of shadows good underdrawers for
owls.
First-plucked before and since the Flood, old hypno-
tisms wrench the golden boughs. Leaves spatter dawn from
emerald cloud-sprockets. Fat final prophets with lean ban-
dits crouch: and dusk is close
                    under your noon,
                    you Sun-heap, whose
ripe apple-lanterns gush history, recondite lightnings, irised.
                    O mister Señor
                    missus Miss
                    Mademoiselle
                    with baskets
                              Maggy, come on

ISLAND QUARRY

Square sheets—they saw the marble only into
Flat prison slabs there at the marble quarry
At the turning of the road around the roots of the
    mountain
5 Where the straight road would seem to ply below the
    stone, that fierce
Profile of marble spiked with yonder
Palms against the sunset's towering sea, and maybe
Against mankind. It is at times—

10 In dusk, as though this island lifted, floated
In Indian baths. At Cuban dusk the eyes
Walking the straight road toward thunder—
This dry road silvering toward the shadow of the
    quarry
15 —It is at times as though the eyes burned hard and glad
And did not take the goat path quivering to the right,
Wide of the mountain—thence to tears and sleep—
But went on into marble that does not weep.

OLD SONG

Thy absence overflows the rose,—
    From every petal gleam
Such words as it were vain to close,
    Such tears as crowd the dream.

5   So eyes that mind thee fair and gone,
    Bemused at waking, spend
On skies that gild thy remote dawn
    More hopes than here attend.

The burden of the rose will fade
10   Sped in the spectrum's kiss.
But here the thorn in sharpened shade
    Weathers all loneliness.

THE IDIOT

Sheer over to the other side,—for see—
The boy straggling under those mimosas, daft
With squint lanterns in his head, and it's likely
Fumbling his sex. That's why those children laughed

5   In such infernal circles round his door
Once when he shouted, stretched in ghastly shape.
I hurried by. But back from the hot shore
Passed him again . . . He was alone, agape;

One hand dealt out a kite string, a tin can
10 The other tilted, peeled end clamped to eye.
That kite aloft—you should have watched him scan
Its course, though he'd clapped midnight to noon sky!

And since, through these hot barricades of green,
A Dios gracias, grac—I've heard his song
15 Above all reason lifting, halt serene—
My trespass vision shrinks to face his wrong.

A NAME FOR ALL

Moonmoth and grasshopper that flee our page
And still wing on, untarnished of the name
We pinion to your bodies to assuage
Our envy of your freedom—we must maim

5   Because we are usurpers, and chagrined—
And take the wing and scar it in the hand.
Names we have, even, to clap on the wind;
But we must die, as you, to understand.

I dreamed that all men dropped their names, and sang
10   As only they can praise, who build their days
With fin and hoof, with wing and sweetened fang
Struck free and holy in one Name always.

BACARDI SPREADS THE EAGLE'S WING

"Pablo and Pedro, and black Serafin
Bought a launch last week. It might as well
Have been made of—well, say paraffin,—
That thin and blistered . . . just a rotten shell.

5   "Hell! out there among the barracudas
Their engine stalled. No oars, and leaks
Oozing a-plenty. They sat like baking Buddhas.
Luckily the Cayman schooner streaks

"By just in time, and lifts 'em high and dry . . .
10 They're back now on that mulching job at Pepper's.
—Yes, patent-leather shoes hot enough to fry
Anyone but these native high-steppers!"

IMPERATOR VICTUS

Big guns again.
No speakee well
But plain.

Again, again—
5   And they shall tell
The Spanish Main

The Dollar from the Cross.

Big guns again.
But peace to thee,
10   Andean brain.

Again, again—
Peace from his Mystery
The King of Spain,

That defunct boss.

15   Big guns again,
Atahualpa,
Imperator Inca—

Slain.

ROYAL PALM

For Grace Hart Crane

Green rustlings, more-than-regal charities
Drift coolly from that tower of whispered light.
Amid the noontide's blazed asperities
I watched the sun's most gracious anchorite

5   Climb up as by communings, year on year
Uneaten of the earth or aught earth holds,
And the grey trunk, that's elephantine, rear
Its frondings sighing in aetherial folds.

Forever fruitless, and beyond that yield
10   Of sweat the jungle presses with hot love
And tendril till our deathward breath is sealed—
It grazes the horizons, launched above

Mortality—ascending emerald-bright,
A fountain at salute, a crown in view—
15   Unshackled, casual of its azured height
As though it soared suchwise through heaven too.

THE AIR PLANT

Grand Cayman

This tuft that thrives on saline nothingness,
Inverted octopus with heavenward arms
Thrust parching from a palm-bole hard by the cove—
A bird almost—of almost bird alarms,

5   Is pulmonary to the wind that jars
Its tentacles, horrific in their lurch.
The lizard's throat, held bloated for a fly,
Balloons but warily from this throbbing perch.

The needles and hack-saws of cactus bleed
10   A milk of earth when stricken off the stalk;
But this,—defenseless, thornless, sheds no blood,
Almost no shadow—but the air's thin talk.

Angelic Dynamo! Ventriloquist of the Blue!
While beachward creeps the shark-swept Spanish Main
15   By what conjunctions do the winds appoint
Its apotheosis, at last—the hurricane!

THE HURRICANE

Lo, Lord, Thou ridest!
Lord, Lord, Thy swifting heart

Naught stayeth, naught now bideth
But's smithereened apart!

5   Ay! Scripture flee'th stone!
Milk-bright, Thy chisel wind

Rescindeth flesh from bone
To quivering whittlings thinned—

Swept—whistling straw! Battered,
10 Lord, e'en boulders now out-leap

Rock sockets, levin-lathered!
Nor, Lord, may worm out-creep

Thy drum's gambade, its plunge abscond!
Lord God, while summits crashing

15 Whip sea-kelp screaming on blond
Sky-seethe, high heaven dashing—

Thou ridest to the door, Lord!
Thou bidest wall nor floor, Lord!

KEY WEST
Folder Subsection

KEY WEST

Here has my salient faith annealed me.
Out of the valley, past the ample crib
To skies impartial, that do not disown me
Nor claim me, either, by Adam's spine—nor rib.

5   The oar plash, and the meteorite's white arch
Concur with wrist and bicep. In the moon
That now has sunk I strike a single march
To heaven or hades—to an equally frugal noon.

Because these millions reap a dead conclusion
10   Need I presume the same fruit of my bone
As draws them towards a doubly mocked confusion
Of apish nightmares into steel-strung stone?

O, steel and stone! But gold was, scarcity before.
And here is water, and a little wind. . . .
15   There is no breath of friends and no more shore
Where gold has not been sold and conscience tinned.

—AND BEES OF PARADISE

I had come all the way here from the sea,
Yet met the wave again between your arms
Where cliff and citadel—all verily
Dissolved within a sky of beacon forms—

5   Sea gardens lifted rainbow-wise through eyes
I found.

           Yes, tall, inseparably our days
Pass sunward. We have walked the kindled skies
Inexorable and girded with your praise,

10 By the dove filled, and bees of Paradise.

TO EMILY DICKINSON

You who desired so much—in vain to ask—
Yet fed your hunger like an endless task,
Dared dignify the labor, bless the quest—
Achieved that stillness ultimately best,

5   Being, of all, least sought for: Emily, hear!
O sweet, dead Silencer, most suddenly clear
When singing that Eternity possessed
And plundered momently in every breast;

—Truly no flower yet withers in your hand.
10   The harvest you descried and understand
Needs more than wit to gather, love to bind.
Some reconcilement of remotest mind—

Leaves Ormus rubyless, and Ophir chill.
Else tears heap all within one clay-cold hill.

MOMENT FUGUE

The syphillitic selling violets calmly
  and daisies
By the subway news-stand knows
    how hyacinths

5 This April morning offers
   hurriedly
In bunches sorted freshly—
     and bestows
On every purchaser
10   (of heaven perhaps)

His eyes—
    like crutches hurtled against glass
Fall mute and sudden (dealing change
  for lilies)
15 Beyond the roses that no flesh can pass.

BY NILUS ONCE I KNEW . . .

Some old Egyptian joke is in the air,
Dear lady—the poet said—release your hair;
Come, search the marshes for a friendly bed
Or let us bump heads in some lowly shed.

5   An old Egyptian jest has cramped the tape.
The keyboard no more offers an escape
From the sweet jeopardy of Anthony's plight:
You've overruled my typewriter tonight.

Decisive grammar given unto queens,—
10   An able text, more motion than machines
Have levers for,—stampede it with fresh type
From twenty alphabets—we're still unripe!

This hieroglyph is no dumb, deaf mistake.
It knows its way through India—tropic shake!
15   It's Titicaca till we've trod it through,
And then it pleads again, "I wish I knew".

TO SHAKESPEARE

Through torrid entrances, past icy poles
 A hand moves on the page! Who shall again
Engrave such hazards as thy might controls—
 Conflicting, purposeful yet outcry vain
5 Of all our days, being pilot,—tempest, too!
 Sheets that mock lust and thorns that scribble hate
Are lifted from torn flesh with human rue,
 And laughter, burnished brighter than our fate
Thou wieldest with such tears that every faction
10 Swears high in Hamlet's throat, and devils throng
Where angels beg for doom in ghast distraction
 —And fail, both! Yet thine Ariel holds his song:
 And that serenity that Prospero gains
 Is justice that has cancelled earthly chains.

POEMS UNCOLLECTED
BUT PUBLISHED
BY CRANE

C 33

He has woven rose-vines
About the empty heart of night,
And vented his long mellowed wines
Of dreaming on the desert white
With searing sophistry.
And he tented with far truths he would form
The transient bosoms from the thorny tree.

O Materna! to enrich thy gold head
And wavering shoulders with a new light shed

From penitence, must needs bring pain,
And with it song of minor, broken strain.
But you who hear the lamp whisper through night
Can trace paths tear-wet, and forget all blight.

OCTOBER–NOVEMBER

Indian-summer-sun
With crimson feathers whips away the mists;
Dives through the filter of trellises
And gilds the silver on the blotched arbor-seats.

5   Now gold and purple scintillate
On trees that seem dancing
In delirium;
Then the moon
In a mad orange flare
10   Floods the grape-hung night.

THE HIVE

Up the chasm-walls of my bleeding heart
Humanity pecks, claws, sobs, and climbs;
Up the inside, and over every part
Of the hive of the world that is my heart.

5   And of all the sowing, and all the tear-tendering,
And reaping, have mercy and love issued forth.
Mercy, white milk, and honey, gold love—
And I watch, and say, "These the anguish are worth."

FEAR

The host, he says that all is well,
And the fire-wood glow is bright;
The food has a warm and tempting smell,—
But on the window licks the night.

5   Pile on the logs. . . . Give me your hands,
Friends! No,—it is not fright. . . .
But hold me . . . somewhere I heard demands. . . .
And on the window licks the night.

ANNUNCIATIONS

The anxious milk-blood in the veins of the earth,
That strives long and quiet to sever the girth
Of greenery. . . . Below the roots, a quickening quiver
Aroused by some light that had sensed,—ere the shiver
Of the first moth's descent,—day's predestiny. . . .
The sound of a dove's flight waved over the lawn. . . .
The moans of travail of one dearest beside me. . . .
Then high cries from great chasms of chaos outdrawn. . . .
Hush! these things were all heard before dawn.

ECHOES

1

Slivers of rain upon the pane,
Jade-green with sunlight, melt and flow
Upward again:—they leave no stain
Of all the storm an hour ago.

2

5   Over the hill a last cloud dips
And disappears, and I should go
As silently but that your lips
Are warmer with a redder glow.

3

Fresh and fragile, your arms now
10   Are circles of cool roses,—so. . . .
In opal pools beneath your brow
I dream we quarreled long, long ago.

THE BATHERS

Two ivory women by a milky sea;—
The dawn, a shell's pale lining restlessly
Shimmering over a black mountain-spear:—
A dreamer might see these, and wake to hear,
But there is no sound,—not even a bird-note;
Only simple ripples flaunt, and stroke, and float,—
Flat lily petals to the sea's white throat.

They say that Venus shot through foam to light,
But they are wrong . . . . Ere man was given sight
She came in such still water, and so nursed
In silence, beauty blessed and beauty cursed.

MODERN CRAFT

Though I have touched her flesh of moons,
Still she sits gestureless and mute,
Drowning cool pearls in alcohol.
O blameless shyness;—innocence dissolute!

5 She hazards jet; wears tiger-lilies;—
And bolts herself within a jewelled belt.
Too many palms have grazed her shoulders:
Surely she must have felt.

Ophelia had such eyes; but she
10 Even, sank in love and choked with flowers.
This burns and is not burnt . . . . My modern love were
Charred at a stake in younger times than ours.

CARMEN DE BOHEME

Sinuously winding through the room
On smokey tongues of sweetened cigarettes,—
Plaintive yet proud the cello tones resume
The andante of smooth hopes and lost regrets.

5   Bright peacocks drink from flame-pots by the wall,
Just as absinthe-sipping women shiver through
With shimmering blue from the bowl in Circe's hall.
Their brown eyes blacken, and the blue drop hue.

The andante quivers with crescendo's start,
10   And dies on fire's birth in each man's heart.
The tapestry betrays a finger through
The slit, soft-pulling:—and music follows cue.

There is a sweep,—a shattering,—a choir
Disquieting of barbarous fantasy.
15   The pulse is in the ears, the heart is higher,
And stretches up through mortal eyes to see.

Carmen! Akimbo arms and smouldering eyes;—
Carmen! Bestirring hope and lipping eyes;—
Carmen whirls, and music swirls and dips.
20   "Carmen!" comes awed from wine-hot lips.

Finale leaves in silence to replume
Bent wings, and Carmen with her flaunts through the gloom
Of whispering tapestry, brown with old fringe:—
The winers leave too, and the small lamps twinge.

25   Morning: and through the foggy city gate
A gypsy wagon wiggles, striving straight.
And some dream still of Carmen's mystic face,—
Yellow, pallid, like ancient lace.

EXILE

(after the Chinese)

My hands have not touched pleasure since your hands,—
No,—nor my lips freed laughter since 'farewell',
And with the day, distance again expands
Voiceless between us, as an uncoiled shell.

5   Yet love endures, though starving and alone.
A dove's wings cling about my heart each night
With surging gentleness, and the blue stone
Set in the tryst-ring has but worn more bright.

POSTSCRIPT

Though now but marble are the marble urns,
Though fountains droop in waning light and pain
Glitters on the edges of wet ferns,
I should not dare to let you in again.

5   Mine is a world foregone though not yet ended,—
An imagined garden grey with sundered boughs
And broken branches, wistful and unmended,
And mist that is more constant than all vows.

FORGETFULNESS

Forgetfulness is like a song
That, freed from beat and measure, wanders.
Forgetfulness is like a bird whose wings are reconciled,
Outspread and motionless,—
5   A bird that coasts the wind unwearyingly.

Forgetfulness is rain at night,
Or an old house in a forest,—or a child.
Forgetfulness is white,—white as a blasted tree,
And it may stun the sybil into prophecy,
10   Or bury the Gods.

I can remember much forgetfulness.

TO PORTAPOVITCH

(du Ballet Russe)

Vault on the opal carpet of the sun,
Barbaric Prince Igor:—or, blind Pierrot,
Despair until the moon by tears be won:—
Or, Daphnis, move among the bees with Chloe.

5   Release,—dismiss the passion from your arms.
More real than life, the gestures you have spun
Haunt the blank stage with lingering alarms,
Though silent as your sandals, danced undone.

LEGENDE

The tossing loneliness of many nights
Rounds off my memory of her.
Like a shell surrendered to evening sands,
Yet called adrift again at every dawn,
5   She has become a pathos,—
Waif of the tides.

The sand and sea have had their way,
And moons of spring and autumn,—
All, save I.
10   And even my vision will be erased
As a cameo the waves claim again.

INTERIOR

It sheds a shy solemnity,
This lamp in our poor room.
O grey and gold amenity,—
Silence and gentle gloom!

5 Wide from the world, a stolen hour
We claim, and none may know
How love blooms like a tardy flower
Here in the day's after-glow.

And even should the world break in
10 With jealous threat and guile,
The world, at last, must bow and win
Our pity and a smile.

PORPHYRO IN AKRON

Greeting the dawn,
A shift of rubber workers presses down
South Main.
With the stubbornness of muddy water
5   It dwindles at each cross-line
Until you feel the weight of many cars
North-bound, and East and West,
Absorbing and conveying weariness,—
Rumbling over the hills.

10 Akron, "high place",—
A bunch of smoke-ridden hills
Among rolling Ohio hills.

The dark-skinned Greeks grin at each other
In the streets and alleys.
15 The Greek grins and fights with the Swede,—
And the Fjords and the Aegean are remembered.

The plough, the sword,
The trowel,—and the monkey wrench!
O City, your axles need not the oil of song.
20 I will whisper words to myself
And put them in my pockets.
I will go and pitch quoits with old men
In the dust of a road.

II

And some of them "will be Americans",
25 Using the latest ice-box and buying Fords;
And others,—

       I remember one Sunday noon,
Harry and I, "the gentlemen",—seated around
A table of raisin-jack and wine, our host
30 Setting down a glass and saying,—

       "One month,—I go back rich.
I ride black horse. . . . Have many sheep."
And his wife, like a mountain, coming in
With four tiny black-eyed girls around her
35 Twinkling like little Christmas trees.

And some Sunday fiddlers,
Roumanian business men,
Played ragtime and dances before the door,
And we overpayed them because we felt like it.

III

40 Pull down the hotel counterpane
And hitch yourself up to your book.

"Full on this casement shone the wintry moon,
And threw warm gules on Madeleine's fair breast,
As down she knelt for heaven's grace and boon . . ."

45 "Connais tu le pays . . . ?"

Your mother sang that in a stuffy parlour
One summer day in a little town
Where you had started to grow.
And you were outside as soon as you
50 Could get away from the company
To find the only rose on the bush
In the front yard. . . . . . .

But look up, Porphyro,—your toes
Are ridiculously tapping
55 The spindles at the foot of the bed.

The stars are drowned in a slow rain,
And a hash of noises is slung up from the street.
You ought, really, to try to sleep,
60 Even though, in this town, poetry's a
Bedroom occupation.

A PERSUASION

If she waits late at night
Hearing the wind,
It is to gather kindnesses
No world can offer.

5 She has drawn her hands away.
The wind plays andantes
Of lost hopes and regrets,—
And yet is kind.

Below the wind,
10 Waiting for morning
The hills lie curved and blent
As now her heart and mind.

THREE LOCUTIONS DES PIERROTS

from the French of Jules Laforgue

I

Your eyes, those pools with soft rushes,
O prodigal and wholly dilatory lady,
Come now, when will they restore me
The orient moon of my dapper affections?

5   For imminent is that moment when,
Because of your perverse austerities,
My crisp soul will be flooded by a languor
Bland as the wide gaze of a Newfoundland.

Ah, madame! truly it's not right
10 When one isn't the real Gioconda,
To adaptate her methods and deportment
For snaring the poor world in a blue funk.

II

Ah! the divine infatuation
That I nurse for Cydalise
Now that she has fled the capture
Of my lunar sensibility!

5   True, I nibble at despondencies
Among the flowers of her domain
To the sole end of discovering
What is her unique propensity!

—Which is to be mine, you say?
10 Alas, you know how much I oppose
A stiff denial to postures
That seem too much impromptu.

154

III

Ah! without the moon, what white nights,
What nightmares rich with ingenuity!
Don't I see your white swans there?
Doesn't someone come to turn the knob?

5   And it's your fault that I'm this way.
That my conscience sees double,
And my heart fishes in troubled water
For Eve, Gioconda, and Dalila.

Oh, by the infinite circumflex
10   Of the archbeam of my cross-legged labours,
Come now,—appease me just a little
With the why-and-wherefore of Your Sex!

THE GREAT WESTERN PLAINS

The little voices of prairie dogs
are tireless . . .
They will give three hurrahs
alike to stage, equestrian, and pullman,
5   and all unstintingly as to the moon.

And Fifi's bows and poodle ease
whirl by them centred in the lap
of Lottie Honeydew, movie queen,
toward lawyers and Nevada.

10   And how much more they cannot see!
Alas, there is so little time,
the world moves by so fast these days!
Burrowing in silk is not their way—
and yet they know the tomahawk.

15   Indeed, old memories come back to life;
pathetic yelps have sometimes greeted
noses pressed against the glass.

AMERICA'S PLUTONIC ECSTASIES

with homage to E. E. Cummings

preferring laxatives to wine
all america is saying
"how are my bowels today?" and
feeling them in every way and
5   peering
for the one goat (unsqueezable)
that kicked out long ago—

or, even thinking
of something—Oh!
10   unbelievably—Oh!
HEADY!—those aromatic LEMONS!
that make your colored syrup fairly
PULSE!—yes, PULSE!

the nation's lips are thin and fast
15   with righteousness. Yet if
memory serves there is still
catharsis from gin-daisies as well as
maiden-hair ferns, and the BRONX
doesn't stink at all

20   These
and other natural grammarians are ab-
so-loot-lee necessary
for a FREE-ER PASSAGE—(NOT
to india, o ye faithful,
25   but a little BACK DOOR DIGNITY)

INTERLUDIUM

To "La Montagne" by Lachaise

Thy time is thee to wend
with languor such as gains
immensity in gathered grace; the arms
to spread; the hands to yield their shells

5   and fostering
thyself, bestow to thee
illimitable and unresigned
(no instinct flattering vainly now)

Thyself
10   that heavens climb to measure, thus
unfurling thee untried,—until
from sleep forbidden now and wide
partitions in thee—goes

communicant and speeding new
15   the cup again wide from thy throat to spend
those streams and slopes untenanted thou
hast known . . . . And blithe

Madonna, natal to thy yielding
still subsist I, wondrous as
20   from thine open dugs shall still the sun
again round one more fairest day.

MARCH

Awake to the cold light
of wet wind running
twigs in tremors. Walls
are naked. Twilights raw—
5 and when the sun taps steeples
their glistenings dwindle
upward . . .

      March
slips along the ground
10 like a mouse under pussy-
willows, a little hungry.

The vagrant ghost of winter,
is it this that keeps the chimney
busy still? For something still
15 nudges shingles and windows:

but waveringly,—this ghost,
this slate-eyed saintly wraith
of winter wanes
and knows its waning.

THE BROKEN TOWER

The bell-rope that gathers God at dawn
Dispatches me as though I dropped down the knell
Of a spent day—to wander the cathedral lawn
From pit to crucifix, feet chill on steps from hell.

5   Have you not heard, have you not seen that corps
Of shadows in the tower, whose shoulders sway
Antiphonal carillons launched before
The stars are caught and hived in the sun's ray?

The bells, I say, the bells break down their tower;
10   And swing I know not where. Their tongues engrave
Membrane through marrow, my long-scattered score
Of broken intervals . . . And I, their sexton slave!

Oval encyclicals in canyons heaping
The impasse high with choir. Banked voices slain!
15   Pagodas, campaniles with reveilles outleaping—
O terraced echoes prostrate on the plain! . . .

And so it was I entered the broken world
To trace the visionary company of love, its voice
An instant in the wind (I know not whither hurled)
20   But not for long to hold each desperate choice.

My word I poured. But was it cognate, scored
Of that tribunal monarch of the air
Whose thigh embronzes earth, strikes crystal Word
In wounds pledged once to hope,—cleft to despair?

25   The steep encroachments of my blood left me
No answer (could blood hold such a lofty tower
As flings the question true?)—or is it she
Whose sweet mortality stirs latent power?—

And through whose pulse I hear, counting the strokes
30 My veins recall and add, revived and sure
The angelus of wars my chest evokes:
What I hold healed, original now, and pure . . .

And builds, within, a tower that is not stone
(Not stone can jacket heaven)—but slip
35 Of pebbles,—visible wings of silence sown
In azure circles, widening as they dip

The matrix of the heart, lift down the eye
That shrines the quiet lake and swells a tower . . .
The commodious, tall decorum of that sky
40 Unseals her earth, and lifts love in its shower.

POEMS UNPUBLISHED
BY CRANE

A SONG FOR HAPPY FEAST DAYS

A song for happy feast days,
A song for fortune's spurns,
In merry and consoling lays—
The cheery songs of Bobbie Burns.

SONNET

Ere elfish Night shall sift another day
Hope-broken 'neath her ebon scepter's keep,
Or the fainting soul's last flames all trembling creep
White-taper-like, and paler, pulse away,
5   Then shalt thou come, O Saint, in magic sway
Of midnight's purple organ-breath, and sweep
Brave echoes from the spooming coast to steep,
Blue heights where cone-wood calls near summits spray
Frost-fringes through thine octaves. . . . And from shades
10   Of moon-fled valleys, there shall rise a rift,
The supplication of all earth, mute serenades,
Whispering, "Cecilia, Saint, leave us thy gift."
And sleep shalt thou bestow, the final song,
And Time shall set the morning stars adrift.

THE MOTH THAT GOD MADE BLIND

Among cocoa-nut palms of a far oasis,
Conceived in the light of Arabian moons,
There are butterflies born in mosaic date-vases,
That emerge black and vermeil from yellow cocoons.

5   Some say that for sweetness they cannot see far,—
That their land is too gorgeous to free their eyes wide
To horizons which knife-like would only mar
Their joy with a barren and steely tide—

That they only can see when their moon limits vision,
10 Their mother, the Moon, marks a halo of light
On their own small oasis, ray-cut, an incision,
Where are set all the myriad jewelleries of night.

So they sleep in the shade of black palm-bark at noon,
Blind only in day, but remembering that soon
15 She will flush their hid wings in the evening to blaze
Countless rubies and tapers in the oasis' blue haze.

But over one moth's eyes were tissues at birth
Too multiplied even to center his gaze
On that circle of paradise cool in the night;—
20 Never came light through that honey-thick glaze.

And had not his pinions with signs mystical
And rings macrocosmic won envy as thrall,
They had scorned him, so humbly low, bound there and tied
At night like a grain of sand, futile and dried.

25 But once though, he learned of that span of his wings,—
The florescence, the power he felt bud at the time
When the others were blinded by all waking things;
And he ventured the desert,—his wings took the climb.

And lo, in that dawn he was pierroting over,—
30 Swinging in spirals round the fresh breasts of day.
The moat of the desert was melting from clover
To yellow,—to crystal,—a sea of white spray—

Till the sun, he still gyrating, shot out all white,—
Though a black god to him in a dizzying night;—
35 And without one cloud-car in that wide meshless blue
The sun saw a ruby brightening ever, that flew.

Seething and rounding in long streams of light
The heat led the moth up in octopus arms:
The honey-wax eyes could find no alarms,
40 But they burned thinly blind like an orange peeled white.

And the torrid hum of great wings was his song
When below him he saw what his whole race had shunned—
Great horizons and systems and shores all along
Which blue tides of cool moons were slow shaken and sunned.

45 A little time only, for sight burned as deep
As his blindness before had frozen in Hell,
And his wings atom-withered,—gone,—left but a leap:—
To the desert,—back,—down,—still lonely he fell.

I have hunted long years for a spark in the sand;—
50 My eyes have hugged beauty and winged life's brief spell.
These things I have:—a withered hand;—
Dim eyes;—a tongue that cannot tell.

TO EARTH

Be earnest, Earth,—and kind.
This flower that opened in the storm
Has fallen with the after-hush.
Be earnest, Earth,—and kind.

MEDUSA

"Fall with me
Through the frigid stars:
Fall with me
Through the raving light:—
5   Sink
Where is no song
But only the white hair of aged winds.

Follow
Into utterness,
10   Into dizzying chaos,—
The eternal boiling chaos
Of my locks!

Behold thy lover,—
Stone!"

MEDITATION

I have drawn my hands away
Toward peace and the grey margins of the day.
The andante of vain hopes and lost regret
Falls like slow rain that whispers to forget,—
Like a song that neither questions nor replies
It laves with coolness tarnished lips and eyes.

I have drawn my hands away
At last to touch the ungathered rose. O stay,
Moment of dissolving happiness! Astir
Already in the sky, night's chorister
Has brushed a petal from the jasmine moon,
And the heron has passed by, alas, how soon!

I have drawn my hands away
Like ships for guidance in the lift and spray
Of stars that urge them toward an unknown goal.
Drift, O wakeful one, O restless soul,
Until the glittering white open hand
Of heaven thou shalt read and understand.

EPISODE OF HANDS

The unexpected interest made him flush.
Suddenly he seemed to forget the pain,—
Consented,—and held out
One finger from the others.

5   The gash was bleeding, and a shaft of sun
That glittered in and out among the wheels,
Fell lightly, warmly, down into the wound.

And as the fingers of the factory owner's son,
That knew a grip for books and tennis
10 As well as one for iron and leather,—
As his taut, spare fingers wound the gauze
Around the thick bed of the wound,
His own hands seemed to him
Like wings of butterflies
15 Flickering in sunlight over summer fields.

The knots and notches,—many in the wide
Deep hand that lay in his,—seemed beautiful.
They were like the marks of wild ponies' play,—
Bunches of new green breaking a hard turf.

20 And factory sounds and factory thoughts
Were banished from him by that larger, quieter hand
That lay in his with the sun upon it.
And as the bandage knot was tightened
The two men smiled into each other's eyes.

THE BRIDGE OF ESTADOR

&&&&

An Impromptu,
Aesthetic
TIRADE

Walk high on the bridge of Estador,
No one has ever walked there before.
There is a lake, perhaps, with the sun
Lapped under it,—or the dun
5   Bellies and estuaries of warehouses,
Tied bundle-wise with cords of smoke.

Do not think too deeply, and you'll find
A soul, an element in it all.

How can you tell where beauty's to be found?
10   I have heard hands praised for what they made;
I have heard hands praised for line on line;
Yet a gash with sunlight jerking through
A mesh of belts down into it, made me think
I had never seen a hand before.
15   And the hand was thick and heavily warted.

High on the bridge of Estador
Where no one has ever been before,—
I do not know what you'll see,—your vision
May slumber yet in the moon, awaiting
20   Far consummations of the tides to throw
Clean on the shore some wreck of dreams. . . .

But some are twisted with the love
Of things irreconcilable,—
The slant moon with the slanting hill:

25   O Beauty's fool, though you have never
Seen them again, you won't forget.
Nor the Gods that danced before you
When your fingers spread among stars.

And you others,—follow your arches
30   To what corners of the sky they pull you to,—
The everlasting eyes of Pierrot,
    Or, of Gargantua, the laughter.

AFTER JONAH

In my beginning was the memory, somehow
contradicting Jonah, that essential babe
of unbaptised digestion, being a nugget
to call pity on Jerusalem and on Nature, too.

5   We have his travels in the snare so widely
ruminated,—of how he stuck there, was reformed,
forgiven, also—
and belched back like a word to grace us all.

There is no settling tank in God. It must be borne
10   that even His bowels are too delicate to board
a sniping thief that has a pious beard.
We must hail back the lamb that went unsheared.

O sweet deep whale as ever reamed the sky
with high white gulfs of vapor, castigate
15   our sins, but be hospitable as Hell.
And keep me to the death like ambergris,
sealed up, and unforgiven in my cell.

EUCLID AVENUE

To be or not to be—?

But so to be the denizen stingaree—
As stertorous as nations romanized may throw
Surveys by Maytimes slow. . . . Hexameters
Suspending jockstraps for gangsters while the pil-

5   Bland (grim)aces Plutarch's perch. And angles
Break in folds of crêpe that blackly drape
The broken door . . . Crouch so. Amend

Then; and clinch.

Sweep. . . .
10   Clean is that cloven Hoof. Then reap
Strain, clasp oblivion as though Chance
Could absent all answer save the chosen rant.

Stop now, as never, never. Speak

As telegrams continue, write, strike
15   Your scholarship (stop) through broken ribs; jail
(Stripe) answers Euclid. Einstein curves, but does not
Quail. Does Newton take the Eucharist on rail
Nor any boulevard no more? I say . . .

For there are statues, shapes your use
20   Repeals. Youse use. You're prevalent,—prevail!
Youse
Food once more and souse, like all me under sail.
My friends, I never thought we'd fail.

That dirty peacock's pride, once gory God's own story:
25   It didn't belong no more; no, never did glory

Walk on Euclid Avenue, as didn't Wm.
Bleached or blacked, whichever 'twas. What milk
We've put in blasted pigs! I says . . . O, well—

But I say, what a swell chance, boys. No more
30 Cancers, jealousy, tenements or giblets! Death, my boys,
Nor blinkers either—

Four shots at who-knows-how—how

Many-it-was unsupervised

Grabbed right outa my mouth that final chew—
35 Right there on Euclid Avenue.

OF AN EVENING
PULLING OFF A LITTLE EXPERIENCE
(with the english language)

by

NIGHTS

5   EEEEEECCCUUUMMMMMMIIINNNGGGSSS (for short)   69

                  wrists web rythms
    and the poke-
        ,dot smile;
    of Genevive
10   talks

    back

    i KNew,kneW my feet
    ?go on) were an applesauce
               part
15   of yoU belching POCHETTEkeepit
    upyou s,uede
    ballbearing

        celery = grin

    remind of-of la guerre

20   UM
    Trimvirate (creamed dancing bitches)
    corking with Helene, (exactly you make)
    my perpendicularly crowdedPOCKets

        smilepoke

25   ,,besides: which
    April has
    a

179

word to say: classy)eh(!
while blundering fumbiguts gather   accu
30   rate little, O-SO masturbations in/
                                to
fractions of heaven. Hold   tight   bless
worms trilling rimple flock to
sad iron

35   goats of
                   love-
                      semi-colon
                      piping (dash)

WHAT NOTS ?

to chorus of:"O bury me not
                        In the lone prairie-ee,
                        Where the wild coyotes
                        Will how-ow-owl at me!"

What is a What Not
if what is not negates
what is not what
you thought it was   ?

O berenberg not
in Laocoön trot —

No;   what is not
esperanto may well be
Lessing to what
not Guthries
plus pot shot double-
double-you Williams:

so   clams open not
to the naughty What Not   !

What a lot of rot, not what
grandma was hot about,   you
say: so
wot I too.   But

what knots and dots
remind *you* of forget-
me-nots   ?

IN A COURT

His hand changed in the kitchen
by the fire: she moved a little,
like wax against his gaze
that followed flame and transfusion,—
5   every spark meshed white, a part
of his most solemn appetite.

I looked into the kitchen where
they sat.
Breathless I was that peace should come
10   where fat is to be grasped and lean
is clenched,
and fingers are a teeth that taste
and smell.

WITH A PHOTOGRAPH

TO ZELL, NOW BOUND FOR SPAIN

From Brooklyn Heights one sees the bay:
And, anchored at my window sill,
I've often sat and watched all day
The boats stream by against the shrill
5   Manhattan skyline,—endlessly
Their mastheads filing out to sea.

And just so, as you see me here
(Though kodaked somewhat out of focus,
My eyes have still the proper locus)
10   I'm flashing greetings to your pier,
Your ship, your auto-bus in France—
All things on which you glide or prance
Down into sunny Spain, dear Zell.
Good berths, good food and wine as well!

15   I hope to know these wishes a true
Forecasting. Let me hear from you.
Enclose some petals from a wall
Of roses in Castile, or maybe garden stall;
While I'll be waiting at this old address,
20   Dear Aunt, God-mother, Editress!

SUPPLICATION TO THE MUSES
ON A TRYING DAY

"How many dawns, chill from his rippling rest,
The seagull's wings shall—"

Hold it in a high wind. The fender curving over the
breastplate, and all in high gear. I watched to see the
river rise. The forests had all given out their streams
and tributaries. When would the bones of De Soto come
5   down in the wild rinse? And when would Ponce de Leon
remember Hammerfest? . . . There were periods when the
salt-rising bread broke out all over me in heinous sores.
If you can't abuse a machine, why have it! Machines
are made for abuse. . . . Fool-proof! Human beings were never
10 jetted, conceived, articulated, *e*jected, nursed,
spanked, corrected, educated, harangued, married, divorced,
petted, emasculated, loved and damned, jailed and liberated,
besides being plastered, frightened and mangled, pickled
and strangled—THEY were never meant to be abused!

15 Thou art no more than Chinese to me, O Moon! A simian
chorus to you, and let your balls be nibbled by the flirt-
atious hauchinango. The tide would rise—and did. I held
the crupper by a lasso conscripted from white mice tails
spliced to the fore-top gallant. Old Mizzentop rose, but
20 all in vain. It was a wild night among the breakers and
the smooth racoons. All the pistols came dressed in white
lattice, winking as never before; but the prawns held out
till nearly daybreak,—simpering, simpering and equivocating.
By the time I reached Berlin—or was it Shanghai?—there
25 were no more stitches for wounds, nor tortoises for teles-
copes. "What a waste of eternity!" I exclaimed into the ear
of the most celebrated microphone you ever smashed. Then
the wind rose, and I strangled in the embraces of a derelict
aigrette.

30 These dermatologists of Mozambique have got hold of me since.
They say my digits fidget, that I'm but a follicle of my
former fratricide. . . . What shall I do? I
masticate firmly and bite off all my nails. I practise in-
vention / to the brink of intelligibility. I insult all my
35 friends and ride ostriches furiously across the Yukon, while
parrots berate me to the accompaniment of the most chaste
reticules. By all the mystery of Gomorrha, I ask, what can a
gaping gastronomist gather in such a gulch of simulation?!!

ETERNITY

September—remember!
October—all over.

BARBADIAN ADAGE

After it was over, though still gusting balefully,
The old woman and I foraged some drier clothes
And left the house, or what was left of it;
Parts of the roof reached Yucatan, I suppose.
5   She almost—even then—got blown across lots
At the base of the mountain. But the town, the town!

Wires in the streets and Chinamen up and down
With arms in slings, plaster strewn dense with tiles,
And Cuban doctors, troopers, trucks, loose hens . . .
10 The only building not sagging on its knees,
Fernandez' Hotel, was requisitioned into pens
For cotted negroes, bandaged to be taken
To Havana on the first boat through. They groaned.

But was there a boat? By the wharf's old site you saw
15 Two decks unsandwiched, split sixty feet apart
And a funnel high and dry up near the park
Where a frantic peacock rummaged amid heaped cans.
No one seemed to be able to get a spark
From the world outside, but some rumor blew
20 That Havana, not to mention poor Batabanó,
Was halfway under water with fires
For some hours since—all wireless down
Of course, there too.

                              Back at the erstwhile house
25 We shoveled and sweated; watched the ogre sun
Blister the mountain, stripped now, bare of palm,
Everything—and lick the grass, as black as patent
Leather, which the rimed white wind had glazed.

Everything gone—or strewn in riddled grace—
30 Long tropic roots high in the air, like lace.
And somebody's mule steamed, swaying right by the pump,
Good God! as though his sinking carcass there
Were death predestined! You held your nose already
Along the roads, begging for buzzards, vultures . . .
35 The mule stumbled, staggered. I somehow couldn't budge
To lift a stick for pity of his stupor.

For I

Remember still that strange gratuity of horses
—One ours, and one, a stranger, creeping up with dawn
40 Out of the bamboo brake through howling, sheeted light
When the storm was dying. And Sarah saw them, too—
Sobbed, Yes, now—it's almost over. For they know;
The weather's in their noses. There's Don—but that one, white
—I can't account for him! And true, he stood
45 Like a vast phantom maned by all that memoried night
Of screaming rain—Eternity!

Yet water, water!

I beat the dazed mule toward the road. He got that far
And fell dead or dying, but it didn't so much matter.

50 The morrow's dawn was dense with carrion hazes
Sliding everywhere. Bodies were rushed into graves
Without ceremony, while hammers pattered in town.
The roads were being cleared, injured brought in
And treated, it seemed. In due time
55 The President sent down a battleship that baked
Something like two thousand loaves on the way.
Doctors shot ahead from the deck in planes.
The fever was checked. I stood a long time in Mack's talking
New York with the gobs, Guantanamo, Norfolk,—
60 Drinking Bacardi and talking U.S.A.

THE SAD INDIAN

Sad heart, the gymnast of inertia, does not count
Hours, days—and scarcely sun and moon—
The warp is in the woof—and his keen vision
Spells what his tongue has had—and only that—
How more?—but the lash, lost vantage—and the prison
His fathers took for granted ages since—and so he looms

Farther than his sun-shadow—farther than wings
—Their shadows even—now can't carry him.
He does not know the new hum in the sky
And—backwards—is it thus the eagles fly?

HIEROGLYPHIC

Did one look at what one saw
Or did one see what one looked at?

INCOMPLETE WORKS

THIS WAY WHERE NOVEMBER . . .

This way where November takes the leaf
to sow only disfigurement in early snow
mist gained upon the night I delved, surely
as the city took us who can meet and go
5 (who might have parted, keen beyond any sea,
in words which no wings can engender now).

For this there is a beam across my head;
its weight not arched like heaven full, its edge
not bevelled, and its bulk that I accept,
10 triumphing not easily upon the brow . . .

And, margined so, the sun may rise aware
(I must have waited for so devised a day)
of the old woman whistling in her tubs,
and a labyrinth of laundry in the courted sky;
15 while inside, downward passing steps
anon not to white buildings I have seen,
leave me to whispering an answer here
to nothing but this beam that crops my hair.

Vaulted in the welter of the east be read,
20 "These are thy misused deeds."—
And the arms, torn white and mild away, be bled.

THOU CANST READ NOTHING . . .

Thou canst read nothing except through appetite
And here we join eyes in that sanctity
Where brother passes brother without sight,
But finally knows conviviality . . .

5 Go then, unto thy turning and thy blame.
Seek bliss then, brother, in my moment's shame.
All this that baulks delivery through words
Shall come to you through wounds prescribed by swords:

That hate is but the vengeance of a long caress,
10 And fame is pivotal to shame with every sun
That rises on eternity's long willingness . . .
So sleep, dear brother, in my fame, my shame undone.

TO LIBERTY

Out of the seagull cries and wind
On this strange shore I build
The virgin. They laugh to hear
How I endow her, standing
5   Hair mocked by the sea, her lover
A dead sailor that knew
Not even Helen's fame.

Light the last torch in the wall,
The sea wall. Bring her no robes yet.
10   They have not seen her in this harbor;
Eyes widely planted, clear, yet small.
And must they overcome the fog,
Or must we rend our dream?

Provide these manners, this salute
15   The brows feed on, anticipate this sanction.
Things become separate, final—
While I become more whole
Infinite—the gradual all
Which is a laugh at last
20   Struggles

TO THE EMPRESS JOSEPHINE'S STATUE

Martinique

Image of Constancy

You, who contain augmented tears, explosions
Have kissed, caressed the model of the hurricane
Gathered and made musical in feathered fronds
The slit eclipse of moon in palm-lit bonds
5   Deny me not in this sweet Caribbean dawn
You, who have looked back to Leda, who have seen the Swan
In swirling rushes, urged the appointed charge,
Outdid our spies and hoodwink sputum,
Now you may compute your lecheries—
10 As well as I, but not with her,—

I own it still—that sure deliberation—
Leave, leave that Caribbean praise to me
Who claims a devout concentration
To wage you surely out of memory—
15 Your generosity dispose relinquishment and care.
Thy death be sacred to all those who share
Love and the breath of faith, momentous bride
You did not die for conquerors at your side
Nor for that fruit of mating that is widowed pride

A POSTSCRIPT

Friendship agony! words came to me
at last shyly. My only final friends—
the wren and thrush, made solid print for me
across dawn's broken arc. No; yes . . . or were they
5   the audible ransom, ensign of my faith
toward something far, now farther than ever away?

Remember the lavender lilies of that dawn,
their ribbon miles, beside the railroad ties
as one nears New Orleans, sweet trenches by the train
10 after the western desert, and the later cattle country;
and other gratuities, like porters, jokes, roses . . .

Dawn's broken arc! and noon's more furbished room!
Yet seldom was there faith in the heart's right kindness.
There were tickets and alarm clocks. There were counters
    and schedules;
15 and a paralytic woman on an island of the Indies,
Antillean fingers counting my pulse, my love forever.

THE PILLAR AND THE POST

What you may yank up *readiest* Yank—
May not so well serve your purpose as your plaint
When you have no one but the devil—to thank
And you wretched with your clean-limbed taint—

5   Of strangling the Argives of the palms—
      Midas of motion—love those lingering
instants that bespeak a careful manure for all
your progeny—and ask the sun what time it
is before your fingers lose their ten—in biological
10 and betrothèd answer to the ambitious monkey synthesis
      that you adore.

THE VISIBLE THE UNTRUE

to E. O.

Yes, I being
the terrible puppet of my dreams, shall
lavish this on you—
the dense mine of the orchid, split in two.
5   And the fingernails that cinch such
environs?
And what about the staunch neighbor tabulations,
with all their zest for doom?

I'm wearing badges
10   that cancel all your kindness. Forthright
I watch the silver Zeppelin
destroy the sky. To
stir your confidence?
To rouse what sanctions—? toothaches?

15   The silver strophe . . . the canto
bright with myth . . . Such
distances leap landward without
evil smile. And, as for me . . .

The window weight throbs in its blind
20   partition. To extinguish what I have of faith.
Yes, light. And it is always
always, always the eternal rainbow
And it is always the day, the farewell day unkind.

A TRAVELLER BORN

Of sailors—those two Corsicans at Marseille,—
The Dane at Paris and the Spanish abbé
With distance, lizard-like, green as Pernod;
Its cargo drench, its wet inferno
5   Condenses memory. The abbey colonnade, the vesperal fountain—
Oh, sudden apple-math of ripe night fallen!
Concluding handclasp, cider, summer-swollen
Folds, and is folden in the echoing mountain. . . .

Yields and is shielded, wrapt in traffic flame,
10 The One, this crucifix that bears a name
Like Science, and the Pasteur Institute . . .
That home for serums keeps the student mute
Until the Fourteenth of July—
(Contain the Paternosters and waive the West wind by)

15 When midnight to lamp bruised black
That nuisance silhouette unhands me
On the ceiling—the midnight clasp extends
(My shadow to myself)
To all the courtesies of foreign friends—

20 I read it clear of anything that bows
Less of the midnight than that midnight shows
Into intrinsic skeletal sincerity—
Less than the stoker or the pilot knows
More than the statesman or the plowman shows. . . .

25 This rhetoric sincere that blinds its flame
To yield it without smoke, intense and sure
The flower's unwithered in vase with name
And so the traveller's home's a foreign cure

HAVANA ROSE

    Let us strip the desk for action—now we have a horse
in Mexico. . . . That night in Vera Cruz—verily for me "the
True Cross"—let us remember the Doctor and my thoughts,
my humble, fond remembrances of the great bacteriologist.
    . . . The wind, that night, the clamour
5 of incessant shutters, trundle doors—and the cheroot
      watchman—
tiptoeing the successive patio balconies with a typical pis-
      tol—trying to muffle doors—and the
pharos shine—the mid-wind midnight stroke of it, its
      milk-light regularity
above my bath partition through the
lofty, dusty glass—*Cortez—Cortez*—his crumbled palace in the
10 square—the typhus in a trap, the Doctor's rat trap.
Where? Somewhere in Vera Cruz—to bring—to take—
to mix—to ransom—to deduct—*to cure* . . . .
The rats played ring around the rosy (in their basement
      basinette)—the Doctor
slept supposedly in #35—thus in my wakeful watch at
      least—the
15 lighthouse flashed . . . whirled . . . delayed, and struck—
      again, again. Only the Mayans surely slept—
whose references to typhus and whose records
spurred the Doctor into something nigh those
metaphysics that are typhoid plus—and had engaged
him once before to death's beyond and back again
20 —antagonistic wills—into immunity. Tact,
horsemanship, courage were germicides to him . . . .
Poets may not be doctors, but doctors are rare
poets when roses leap like rats—and too,
when rats make rose nozzles of pink death around
25 white teeth. . . .

And during the wait over dinner at La Diana,
the Doctor had said—who was American also—
"You cannot heed the negative—, so might go on
to undeserved doom . . . must therefore loose yourself
within a pattern's mastery that you can conceive, that
you can yield to—by which also you
win and gain that mastery and happiness which
is your own from birth."

30

PURGATORIO

My country, O my land, my friends—
Am I apart,—here from you in a land
Where all your gas lights—faces,—sputum gleam
Like something left, forsaken,—here am I—
And are these stars—the high plateau—the scents
Of Eden—and the dangerous tree—are these
The landscape of confession—and if confession
So absolution? Wake pines—but pines wake here.
I dream the too-keen cider—the too-soft snow.
Where are the bayonets that the scorpion may not grow?
Here quakes of earth make houses fall—
And all my countrymen I see rush toward one stall.
Exile is thus a purgatory—not such as Dante built

But rather like a blanket than a quilt
And I have no decision—is it green or brown
That I prefer to country or to town?
I am unraveled, umbilical anew,
So ring the church bells here in Mexico—
(They ring too obdurately here to need my call)
And what hours they forget to chime I'll know
As one whose altitude at one time was
                    not

202

THE CIRCUMSTANCE

To Xochipilli

The anointed stone, the coruscated crown—
The drastic throne, the
Desperate sweet eyepit-basins of a bloody foreign clown—
Couched on bloody basins floating bone
Of a dismounted people. . . .

If you could buy the stones,
Display the stumbling bones
Urging your unsuspecting
Shins, sus-
Taining nothing in time but more and more of Time,
Mercurially might add but would
Subtract and concentrate. . . . If you
Could drink the sun as did and does
Xochipilli,—as they who've
Gone have done, as they
Who've done. . . . A god of flowers in statued
Stone . . . of love—

If you could die, then starve, who live
Thereafter, stronger than death smiles in flowering stone;—
You could stop time, give florescent
Time a longer answer back (shave lightning,
Possess in halo full the winds of time)
A longer answer force, more enduring answer
As they did—and have done. . . .

FRAGMENTS

TO BUDDHA

You are quite outside of such issues,
The polished bottom of your sound font
Is taught to ride in heaven, and you know
The tangents of desire the other quells

WHERE GABLES PACK . . .

Where gables pack the rainless
fulsome sky
permit a song as comes into the street

permit a song that swings with ropes
and skipping feet
above the laughter that rebounds below.

WELL/WELL/NOT-AT-ALL

Yakka-hoola-hikki-doola
Pico-della-miran-dohhh-la
leonarda-della-itchy-vinci
es braust ein Ruf wie
        DONNERHALL
5   pffffff !

YOU ARE THAT FRAIL . . .

You are that frail decision that devised
Their lowest common multiple of human need,
And on that bleak assumption risked the prize
Forgetfulness of all you bait for greed . . .

THE MASTERS

Their brains are smooth machines that colonize
The sun,—their eyes are atoms of a split hereafter.
They must explain away all moan and laughter,
Then ticket, subdivide and overrule
5   Each former entity *****
I saw them turn old Demos from the stage
And mock their hearts because their hearts spoke better,
Elaborate all, divided school by school

HER EYES HAD . . .

Her eyes had the blue of desperate days,
Freezingly bright; I saw her hair unfurl,
Unsanctioned, finally, by anything left her to know
She had learned that Paradise is not a question of eggs
If anything, it was her privilege to undress
Quietly in a glass she had guarded
Always with correcting states before.

It was this, when I asked her how she died,
That asked me why her final happy cry
Should not have found an echo somewhere, and I stand
Before her finally, as beside a wall, listening as though
I heard the breath of Holofernes toast
Judith's cold bosom through her righteous years.

O MOON, THOU COOL . . .

O moon, thou cool sibilance of the sun, we utmost love
A Quaker in the sky the clouds resign—
For that ye yield one answer, one above
All else of midnight—that we shall not
5   I begged a mediator in thy sign
               thy free industry
Thy leap and petal over the stiff edge
Where no one else dare set the wedge
O the moon crops weather on the spine
10   Of every buckwheat that the bee takes in in his prime
Your mother, sibilance of the sun, is the vine

THE SEA RAISED UP . . .

The sea raised up a campanile . . . The wind I heard
Of brine partaking, whirling into shower
Of column that breakers sheared in shower
Back into bosom,—me—her, into natal power . . .

SO DREAM THY SAILS . . .

So dream thy sails, O phantom bark
That I thy drownèd men may speak again
Perhaps as once Will Collins spoke the lark,
And leave me half adream upon the main.

5   For who shall lift head up to funnel smoke,
And who trick back the leisured winds again
As they were fought—and wooed? They now but stoke
Their vanity, and dream no land in vain.

Of old there was a promise, and thy sails
10   Have kept no faith but wind, the cold stream
—The hot fickle wind, the breath of males
Imprisoned never, no not soot and steam

I HAVE THAT SURE ENCLITIC . . .

I have that sure enclitic to my act
Which shall insure no dissonance to fact.
Then Agamemnon's locks grow to shape
Without my forebear's priceless model of the ape . . . .
5   Gorillas die—and so do humanists—who keep
Comparisons clear for evolution's non-escape
And man the deathless target, of his own weak sheep . . .

SHALL I SUBSUME . . .

Shall I subsume the shadow of the world—
The sun-spot that absolves us all? In fine
There is the wisp, there is the phantom,
"Fantisticon", in the comedy where we meet.
The interlude without circumvention
This, between the speech of shells and battle gases.
I know this effort by the slant of the obdurate moon.
She, at worst, is the chancel—of our worst reflection

Immeasurable scope of veins, imprisoned within mood
Whereon the distance thrives—O jealousy of space!
I, these cameos, carve—thy caverns limitless achieve—
These arteries explore. What is the extent of the sod?
And where is the clod blown up with

TENDERNESS AND RESOLUTION

Tenderness and resolution
What is our life without a sudden pillow—
What is death without a ditch?

The harvest laugh of bright Apollo
And the flint tooth of Sagittarius
Rhyme from the same jaw—(closing cinch by cinch)
And pocket us who, somehow, do not follow,
As though we knew those who are variants—
Charms—that each by each refuse the clinch

With desperate propriety, whose name is writ
In wider letters than the alphabet,—
Who is now left to vary the Sanscrit
Pillowed by

My wrist in the vestibule of time—who
Will hold it—wear the keepsake, dear, of time—
Return the mirage on a coin that spells
Something of sand and sun the Nile defends. . . .

TIME CANNOT BE WORN . . .

Time cannot be worn strapped to the supple wrist
Like any buckled jewel or bangle; no,
Lady, though fingers that attach it twist
The oyster from its shell, may guide the bow
5   Across cool strings that lift a lasting claim
Upon Eternity. No, Lady,

I ROB MY BREAST . . .

I rob my breast to reach those altitudes—
To meet the meaningless concussion of
Pure heights—Infinity resides below. . . .
The obelisk of plain infinity founders below
My vision is a grandiose dilemma—

Place de la Concorde! Across that crowded plain—
I fought to see the stricken bones, the noble
Carcass of a general, dead Foch, proceed
To the defunct pit of Napoleon—in honor
Defender, not usurper.

My countrymen,—give form and edict—
To the marrow. You shall know
The harvest as you have known the spring
But I believe that such "wreckage" as I find
Remaining presents evidence of considerably more
Significance than do the cog-walk gestures
Of a beetle in a sand pit.

ENRICH MY RESIGNATION . . .

Enrich my resignation as I usurp those far
Feints of control—hear rifles blown out on the stag
Below the aeroplane—and see the fox's brush
Whisk silently beneath the red hill's crag
5 —Extinction stirred on either side
Because love wonders, keeps a certain mirth—
Die, Oh, centuries, die, as Dionysius said,
Yet live in all my resignation—
It is the moment, now, when all—
10 The heartstrings spring, unlaced—Oh thou fiend and

Here is the peace of the fathers

ALL THIS . . .

All this—and the housekeeper—
Written on a blotter, Hartford, Bridgeport—
The weekend at Holyoke
His daughters act like kings
5 Pauline and I, the Harvard game
—A brand new platform
Way on Stutzing up to Spring
—Not a cent, not a cent, wish we'd known beforehand.

And the last of the Romanoffs
10 Translated the International Code
Tea and toast across radios
Swung into lullabies.
His father gave him the store outright
—All sorts of money, Standard Oil
15 And his two sons, their fourth or fifth cousins
How well he carried himself
And a stick all the time

THE ALERT PILLOW . . .

The alert pillow, the hayseed spreads
And mountains wasting carpet—
O willows, drooping forecast—tears?
That demiurge, turf earns the station
Whereby candles are bought and hymns
Sparkle alone in wastebaskets and whereto
Scythes, those seldom spears—by
Poets urged—so their sunset crescents
Swiftly and like iron sweep acceptance

THERE ARE THE LOCAL . . .

There are the local orchard boughs
With apples—August boughs—their unspilled spines
Inter-wrenched and flocking with gold spousal wine
Like hummocks drifting in the autumn shine

DUST NOW IS . . .

Dust now is the old-fashioned house
Where Jacob dreamed his ladder climb,—
Thankfully fed both hog and mouse
And mounted rung on rung of rhyme

THEY WERE THERE . . .

They were there falling;
And they fell. And their habitat
Left them. And they fell.
And what they remembered was—
Dismembered. But they fell.
And now they dispel
Those wonders that posterity constructs,
By such a mystery as time obstructs;
And all the missions and votaries
And old maids with their chronic coteries
Dispense in the old, old lorgnette views
What should have kept them straight in pews.
But doesn't confuse
These Indians, who scan more news
On the hind end of their flocks each day
Than all these tourists bring their way.

TO CONQUER VARIETY

I have seen my ghost broken
My body blessed
And Eden
Scraped from my mother's breast
5   When the charge was spoken
Love dispossessed
And the seal broken . . . . .

A NOTE ON THE EDITORIAL METHOD

The aim of this edition is to produce a text of the published and unpublished poems of Hart Crane that is as close as possible to his latest intention in his most authoritative form of each poem. Consequently, his latest copy meant for the printer, or the subsequent form of the text closest to that copy, has been chosen as Crane's intended text, for, as modern textual theory recognizes, they are the forms with highest reliability in both micro- and macro-elements. When the printer's copy has not survived—often the case with Crane's poems—the first printing, which is the next closest text to the printer's copy, is used for the text in this edition. If some other form is closer or more reliable, it is discussed in the Notes. Since any incomplete or fragmentary pieces have a less than certain authorial intention inherent in their extant forms, the editor has deduced Crane's intended text according to the poet's usual practice. This criterion is based on careful study of Crane's habits of living and writing, and informed by a complete collation of all Crane's variants in order to determine a text in the absence of a fair copy. It is central, though, that the texts provided here are primarily the author's, not this editor's; nor those of Crane's other editors, whose alterations are not cited unless it is necessary and space allows. This text and its emendations have been shaped, however, by a critical interpretation of other editors' readings of dubious passages, especially in works that are less than complete. Thus this edition emends defective texts only by using forms which are demonstrably Crane's, or because there is a patent error that he missed that should be corrected.

The editor has not imposed consistency regarding capitalization or punctuation, unless it is clear that such inconsistencies derive from an oversight or from the unauthorized license of editor or compositor. Any need for editorial emendation is justified in the Notes (if the correction is not an obvious one), as is the rationale concerning the *"KEY WEST"* folder. The present edition normalizes the number and spacing of dots if the poet's form is ambiguous or erratic, unless he specifically noted (as in "Cape Hatteras," for example) that his form of the ellipsis should remain intentionally at variance from the norm. Thus the closeup place-

227

ment of four dots represents the period directly after the last quoted word, and the spaced placement (as in three dots) represents an ellipsis that begins in mid-sentence and the fourth dot indicates the final period. Other normalizations are mainly a matter of mechanical presentation. Heading capitals in the first line of a poem or section of a poem are silently altered in this edition. Line- and page-breaks, if they obscure stanzaic structure and are clearly a result only of house style, are altered—and discussed in the Notes when need be. All digraphs have been emended, since they are the imposition of house style. Anomalous typographical usage has been normalized when it does not originate in Crane's documents, or if it is inconsequential, such as the upper- or lower-case letters of a title and final periods in titles or sections of poems. Line counts for separate poems are literal and consecutive; one word counts as a line if it is written as a line in Crane's last extant version. Poems part of a series, such as the sections of "For the Marriage of Faustus and Helen," "Voyages," or *THE BRIDGE*, are line-numbered separately (and not continuously from first to last section of the poem) for reasons of convenience rather than because of assumptions about such sequences of poems as more or less unified.

Notes

Br THE BRIDGE A Poem by HART CRANE (New York: Horace
Liveright, 1930).
c. circa, about
HC   Hart Crane
WB   White Buildings: Poems by Hart Crane (New York: Boni & Liveright,
1926).

In order to afford precise distinctions for the reader's recognition of HC's
development as an artist in light of his complete as well as not finished
work, the editor has grouped *The Poems of Hart Crane* into seven parts,
along with Notes on dates of composition and first publication by HC,
and other relevant information regarding the source of each poem, edi-
torial emendation of the poems, and explanations of significant critical
elements as space allows. The first two sections consist of HC's two
separately published books. The next five parts comprise complete,
incomplete, and fragmentary works. By distinguishing incomplete works
from fragments, one soon realizes that HC left the former in a relatively
finished if not complete fair-copy form compared to his verse fragments.
HC gave titles to all the incomplete works except those which begin
"This Way Where November . . ." and "Thou Canst Read Nothing . . ." .
To only four of the fragments did HC give titles. One of them, "The
Masters," HC himself designated as a "fragment note," while the other
three are only pieces or fragments of works that he never developed. The
grouping of incomplete works apart from fragments provides the dis-
crimination necessary for the reader's immediate comprehension of, and
insight into, HC's incomplete works *as* such, and his fragments such as
they are, namely parts of works that have survived in not even an incom-
plete form.

   Therefore, HC's intentions for sequence of publication of his major
works in separate book form are accorded primacy, and his third tenta-
tive book or section of a book of collected poems follows (with justifica-
tion in the Notes). Although it is not known what HC would have done
with his incomplete works and fragments, in the absence of his clear
intentions, they are grouped after his purposely separate publications

(White Buildings and *THE BRIDGE)*, a provisionally distinct collection
(*"KEY WEST"*), poems published individually but uncollected by him,
and works he did not publish himself. Thus *The Poems of Hart Crane*
presents each text according to the place it takes along a continuum vary-
ing from separate publications to fragments. Such a sequence comes clos-
est to how HC would have intended his editor to present his extant
compositions to future readers eager to have for the first time the com-
plete canon of all his ninety-two poems (besides those in HC's two books
published in his lifetime) available in one volume.

White Buildings

The text of this edition is based on the first impression of *WB*. HC
expressed his complete satisfaction with this first printing, and no evi-
dence suggests that he sought to revise or correct it after publication. If
no date of first publication of a poem appears in the following Notes,
HC did not publish it except in *WB* or in the first edition of *THE BRIDGE*,
as the case may be. When months for publication dates are omitted it is
because the date is vague, e.g., September–December. Epigraph: "RIM-
BAUD" emends "RIMBAUD." The period is house style, not HC's.

LEGEND

Composed 1924; first published September 1925.

BLACK TAMBOURINE

Composed 1921; first published June 1921.

EMBLEMS OF CONDUCT

Composed *c.* late 1923–early 1924.

MY GRANDMOTHER'S LOVE LETTERS

Composed *c.* November–December 1919; first published April 1920. Line
1: "tonight" emends "to-night". The hyphenated spelling is house style,
not HC's. The poet used "to-night" nowhere in his typewritten or auto-
graph manuscripts of this or his other poems.

NOTES TO PAGES 7–14 | 231

SUNDAY MORNING APPLES

Composed 1922; first published July 1924.

PRAISE FOR AN URN

Composed 1921–1922; first published June 1922.

GARDEN ABSTRACT

Composed and first published 1920.

STARK MAJOR

Composed and first published 1923. Line 17: "you," emends "you" on the basis of all HC's extant documents of the poem that precede the *WB* proofs. The syntax also suggests the need for the emendation with a comma, which *WB* also omits.

CHAPLINESQUE

Composed *c*. October–November 1921; first published December 1921.

PASTORALE

Composed *c*. July 1921; first published October 1921.

IN SHADOW

Composed *c*. September 1917; first published December 1917.

THE FERNERY

Composed *c*. April–December 1920–*c*. 1921. First published September 1922.

NORTH LABRADOR

Composed *c.* September 1917; first published November 1919.

REPOSE OF RIVERS

Composed *c.* early 1926; first published September 1926.

PARAPHRASE

Composed *c.* October 1924; first published September 1925.

POSSESSIONS

Composed *c.* September 1923–*c.* March 1924; first published Spring 1924.

LACHRYMAE CHRISTI

Composed *c.* February 1924–*c.* early April 1925; first published December 1925. Line 26: "eyes" marks the end of a one-line stanza, which is not clear in some printings of the poem.

PASSAGE

Composed *c.* August–December 1925; first published July 1926.

THE WINE MENAGERIE

Composed *c.* October 1925–April 1926; first published May 1926.

RECITATIVE

Composed October 1923–*c.* March 1924; first published Spring 1924.

FOR THE MARRIAGE OF FAUSTUS AND HELEN

Composed March 1921–*c*. late 1923. Parts were first published January and September 1923 and Winter 1924. Part 2, line 4: "opéra" emends "opera". Part 3, line 21: "air!" marks the end of the stanza, which some printings of the poem leave unclear.

AT MELVILLE'S TOMB

Composed October 1925; first published July 1926.

VOYAGES, I, II, III, IV, V, VI

Composed *c*. October 1921–April 1926; first published in part in January 1923 and Spring 1926. "Voyages IV" line 9: "irrefragably" emended from "irrefragibly", which is a misspelling overlooked by HC and the publishers of *WB*. There is no evidence that "HC may have had the relevant adverb 'irrefrangibly' in mind when he wrote 'irrefragibly' " (Brom Weber, ed. *The Complete Poems and Selected Letters and Prose of Hart Crane* [New York: Liveright, 1966], p. 277).

Line 15: "today" emends "to-day". The hyphen was most likely introduced as house style, since "today" appears in all HC's documents of the form before the *WB* proofs.

THE BRIDGE

This edition's text is based on the proofs corrected in HC's hand for the first impression of the second edition of *Br*, which is the latest version with his alterations. HC preferred the second edition over the first edition (Paris: The Black Sun Press, 1930). Since no printer's copy survives, the proofs of *Br* are the next most reliable source before the second edition, first impression of the poem, which varies from the proofs of *Br*.

TO BROOKLYN BRIDGE

Composed and revised *c*. July 1926–*c*. January 1930; first published June 1927. The proofs of the first edition, and the first edition of *THE BRIDGE* itself, have the poem in italics from title to last word. In the proofs of *Br* the poem is set in italic type except for the second line of the title. However, HC's intentions were thwarted after he noted in the proofs of *Br* in ink in the margins that the italic "type is too small" in some of the lines.

The proofs of *Br* have pencil directions not in HC's hand that the text of the poem after the title be "Reset in Roman, same as balance of book", which was done in *Br*. HC's intended italic version has been reinstated in the present edition.

AVE MARIA

Composed and revised *c.* January 1926–*c.* August 1929; first published 1927. Epigraph, line 4: *"Tethysque"* (in the first edition) is used to emend *"Tiphysque"* or its variant in all other versions because of the following: Below the epigraph in the first edition proofs "look up in Medea?" is inscribed and circled in pencil, but not in HC's hand. The form *"Tiphysque"* became *"Tethysque"* in the first edition, but HC had not changed or commented on the quotation, which he had taken from an inaccurate source. Tethys was "the sister and wife of Oceanus, often personifying the sea." Tiphyn was "the helmsman of the Argo" who "died of a sickness while the Argonauts were . . . in Bithynia" (see Seneca, *Medea*, ed. C.D.N. Costa [London: Oxford University Press, 1973] nn. 3, 318, 377). Contrariwise, see R.W.B. Lewis, *Hart Crane* (Princeton: Princeton University Press, 1967), pp. 49 n., 257–258.

Line 50: "lee!" at the end of the line is followed by three spaced dots centered below the line. In a *c.* summer–fall 1926 typescript of the poem HC has the same space above and below the dots after lines 50 and 56. But in a January 1927 typescript of "Ave Maria" and in his other documents of the poem which follow, HC clearly intended lines 49–56 as one stanza, with three dots below line 50; and the dots below line 56 he consistently set with more space above and below to indicate a stanza-break. The distinction was obscured by the printing of the poem in *The American Caravan* in 1927, which likely made him more sensitive to the matter, since in his *c.* July–August 1929 typed and handwritten manuscript HC noted "generous space here" between lines 56–57. In the proofs of *Br* he overlooked the spacing because page 12 ended with line 46, which broke the stanza and blurred the spatial distinction in the proofs, whereas the first edition proofs had printed both stanzas on one page and thus the difference was more obvious. HC's intended "generous space" between lines 56–57 for the clarification of the stanza-break is restored in the present edition.

THE HARBOR DAWN

Composed and revised late 1926–*c.* January 1930; first published June 1927. In the proofs of *Br* corrected in HC's hand in ink, the glosses were all printed to the right, as he intended. He had placed them to the right whenever they were included in his documents of *THE BRIDGE* before the proofs of *Br*. However, the second, third, and fourth glosses in "The Harbor Dawn," the first and third in "The River," and the one gloss in "The Dance" were moved in the proofs of *Br* by graphite pencil lines in a hand other than HC's that indicate that they be printed to the left of the text so that they would be on the unbound side of *Br*. In the present edition, all the glosses are to the right of the text, as HC intended. HC had corrected the proofs of *Br* only in blue-black ink, not in pencil, and clearly intended the glosses as afterwords and not as preliminary comments on the text of the poems, even if it meant that they sometimes would appear in the bound margins of the volume. The evidence suggests that HC's intentions were overridden in *Br* and its second impression in which the glosses, when placed on the verso of any page, are to the left of the text, or he acquiesced in the Liveright choice. Thus the proofs as printed and corrected by HC for *Br*, not as altered by a hand other than HC's, provide the basis for the placement of the glosses in the present edition. The gloss between lines 31–32 (based on HC's documents and explicit instructions before the proofs of *Br*) emends the gloss from opposite line 32.

In the proofs of *Br* the title-page epigraphs in whole or part have also been moved left or right in red or graphite pencil by a hand other than HC's before "Cape Hatteras," "Quaker Hill," "The Tunnel," and "Atlantis." The present edition in this matter follows the proofs as printed for *Br* rather than as altered by the Liveright staff.

VAN WINKLE

Composed and revised *c*. February 1923–*c*. August 1929; first published October 1927.

THE RIVER

Composed and revised between *c*. late June–August 1926 and *c*. August 1929; first published 1928. The second gloss in the proofs of *Br*, and in *Br* itself begins opposite line 27, which is emended to line 28, where HC typed it explicitly on the gloss sheet sent to Caresse Crosby for the first edition, rather than his merely having marked a line with an "x" after line 29, as he did in other documents of the poem. None of HC's autograph or typewritten manuscripts of the poem indicates that the gloss follow line 27, but in his two final typescripts of the poem the gloss follows line 28.

THE DANCE

Composed and revised between *c*. July–August 1926 and *c*. September 1929; first published October 1927.

INDIANA

Composed and revised *c*. September 1927 and between *c*. September–October 1929 and *c*. January 1930.

CUTTY SARK

Composed and revised *c*. July 1926–September 1929; first published June 1927. The terminal punctuation in lines 72, 82, 84, and 85 is emended from italic to roman because HC intended to italicize only the names of the ships. All his original documents of the poem support these changes.

CAPE HATTERAS

Composed *c*. March 1926–September 1929. Line 19: "Pocahontas" emends "Pocahuntus" because the former is consistent with HC's form of the name in "The Dance" (lines 14, 52). It contrasts with what HC termed the "antique spelling ["Pocahuntus"] of the quotation" used as an epigraph to "Powhatan's Daughter." HC also used this edition's spelling of the name in line 19 in one of his late typewritten and autograph documents as well as in the first edition of the poem.

Line 53: "cliff," emends "cliff." The comma was altered in pencil to a period in the proofs of *Br*, but not in HC's hand. All HC's documents before the proofs of *Br* have "cliff," in this line. Lines 198, 228: HC intended to italicize only the Latin phrase, as in line 209, and thus the exclamation marks are emended from italic to roman, which is supported by four of his original documents for line 198, and by five for line 228.

Stanza breaks: none at lines 191 and 222.

SOUTHERN CROSS

Composed and revised *c*. August 1926–*c*. January 1930; first published 1927.

NATIONAL WINTER GARDEN

Composed and revised *c*. summer 1926–*c*. January 1930; first published 1927.

VIRGINIA

Composed and revised *c.* August 1926–*c.* January 1930; first published 1927.

QUAKER HILL

Composed between *c.* June–July 1927 and *c.* December 1929.

THE TUNNEL

Composed and revised *c.* first half of 1926–*c.* July 1929; first published November 1927.

ATLANTIS

Composed *c.* February 1923–*c.* December 1929. Line 76 was inadvertently omitted from the proof of *Br* at the bottom of its page 81 but restored in *Br*, which is the source for the line in the present edition. The line also appears in Crane's original documents of the poem.

KEY WEST   An Island Sheaf

The basis for the text in the present edition is the latest version of each poem in HC's *"KEY WEST"* manila folder with thirty-two unnumbered sheets. One exception is "Bacardi Spreads the Eagle's Wing," the text of which is discussed below.

HC wrote Yvor Winters on 18 July 1927 from Patterson, N.Y., about

> the Carib suite that I've been meditating. (It's rather good to get off the Bridge for awhile) [stet]. Two remain to be written, but I think I'll group them together under the common title of *The Hurricane*, beginning with
>
> O Carib Isle!
> Quarry
> The Air Plant
> Royal Palm
> The Idiot (still to be written)
>   & Eternity (a description of the ruins)
> with maybe one or two more items
> as my tropical memories dictate.[1]

From May to late October 1926, HC had been in the Caribbean, mainly on the Isle of Pines, which he had also visited in January–February 1915 with his parents as a youth. He had left the Isle of Pines after a hurricane in early October 1926. His meditations in the Caribbean before 19 June 1926 had already produced "The Mango Tree," and on that date he reported to Waldo Frank that "I'm cooking up a couple of other short poems to go with it ('Kidd's Cove,' & 'The Tampa Schooner') under the common title of 'Grand Cayman.' "[2] On 12 July [1927] he had sent Winters an early form of "The Air Plant," "meant along with two or three others as a companion piece to Carib Isle."[3]

When he wrote Frank on 1 February 1928 from Altadena, California, the idea of a group of poems that were "souvenirs of [their] . . . sojourn together" in early May 1926 to the Isle of Pines preoccupied HC as he considered what would later be entitled "Bacardi Spreads the Eagle's Wing" and "The Hurricane" as also "properly belonging to this series"[4] of poems earlier listed for Winters. Thus by early 1928 he had already tentatively prepared a series of eight thematically related poems for eventual publication together.

The "CONTENTS" table of the *"KEY WEST"* folder attests to HC's intention to publish the folder's group of thirteen poems as a sequence under the title *"KEY WEST."* However, the six poems entitled "Key West," "—And Bees of Paradise," "To Emily Dickinson," "Moment Fugue," "By Nilus Once I Knew . . . ," and "To Shakespeare" are not in the "CONTENTS" after the thirteen titles, but are in the *"KEY WEST"* manila folder, and thus are presented as a subsection of the poems in the *"KEY WEST"* folder in the present edition, since no evidence suggests that the *"Sheaf"* was not an inchoate third book of poems. Thus the poems in the folder are presented in the form and order in which they have survived, in the absence of authorial evidence attesting to any other canon and ordonnance. Alan Howard Schwartz has suggested that the sheets of the folder may have been altered in their sequence or added into the folder, or even possibly removed from it in the case of a poem like "The Broken Tower."[5] The correspondence of Grace Hart Crane, Samuel Loveman, and Waldo Frank suggests otherwise; namely, that they were careful not to alter the ordonnance of HC's papers from that which the documents had when they received them. Nor is there any evidence that Peggy Baird had placed poems into or out of the folder when she was with Crane in Mexico.

The present edition, however, recognizes that HC did not leave the *"Island Sheaf"* in a final form. Thus the *"KEY WEST"* folder's six poems omitted from the "CONTENTS" are presented in the sequence in which they appear in the folder, and the rest follow the order of the "CONTENTS," which is the same as the order that each poem and its drafts take in the folder itself. The folder's cover is an ink-inscribed variant form of the typewritten title page. The title page and contents page date from between about February 1930 and March 1932. The documents in the folder date from various years indicated in the following notes to each poem.

Though R.W.B. Lewis has remarked that John Unterecker once speculated that the "Key West" poems "would have been the title of only one portion of a later volume of lyrics,"[6] and though Unterecker himself later wrote that in the latter part of 1928 HC was "trying to assemble from the Isle of Pines material a substantial section of a new volume,"[7] the following evidence implies an alternate conclusion. On 5 May 1932, Glenn Whistler, long a friend of the poet and his mother, wrote Mrs. Crane:

> I saw Hart several times about a year ago . . . He seemed in good
> spirits—and shortly after that he received the Guggenheim Award.
> He said that his next book would be made up of various short poems.[8]

On 13 May 1932, Malcolm Cowley wrote Grace Hart Crane that her son had told him "before he died that he had poems enough among his papers for a small book."[9] Though "that . . . small book" was never published by HC, it survived in preliminary form in the "*KEY WEST*" folder, and is thus grouped after the "Bridge" section in the present edition. The italicized "*KEY WEST*" title on the manila folder and the title page (with its underlined half-title) are retained as HC left them, as well as to distinguish the "*Sheaf*" title from the separate "Key West" poem title. The two commas and a period in the Blake epigraph are emended to italic.

NOTES

[1]Typewritten letter signed, quoted by permission of The Bancroft Library. See Thomas Parkinson, *Hart Crane and Yvor Winters Their Literary Correspondence* (Berkeley: University of California Press, 1978), pp. 98–99.

[2]*The Letters of Hart Crane 1916–1932*, ed. Brom Weber (Berkeley: University of California Press, 1965), p. 259.

[3]Parkinson, p. 98.

[4]*Letters*, pp. 315–316.

[5]"Hart Crane's Poetry: A Critical Edition," unpublished dissertation (New York University, 1967), pp. cxxii–cxxx, 218–219.

[6]*The Poetry of Hart Crane* (Princeton: Princeton University Press, 1967), p. 400, n. 13.

[7]*Voyager A Life of Hart Crane* (New York: Farrar, Straus and Giroux, 1969), p. 561.

[8]Unpublished letter.

[9]Unpublished letter.

O CARIB ISLE!

Composed and revised *c.* end of August 1926–*c.* late May 1931; first published April 1927. The present edition takes HC's last version after several earlier documents as the basis for the text. It is sheet 5 in the folder, and has HC's ink emendation.

THE MERMEN

Composed and revised *c.* July 1927–*c.* late 1928; first published September 1928. The present text is based on sheet 6, which has HC's pencil inscription in this latest document of the poem. Epigraph: "*And if*" emends "And if".

TO THE CLOUD JUGGLER

Composed January 1930; first published June 1930. Sheet 7 in the folder provides the present text. No other original HC document of the poem has been located. This one has HC's autograph emendation and another inscription in his hand. Dedication: roman colon emended to italic.

THE MANGO TREE

Composed May 1926–September 1929; first published November 1929. The text is based on sheet 8 in the folder; it is his last version of the poem. The tilde is added in the present text of "Señor" in line 14, since no evidence suggests that HC intended to omit the tilde for ironic or other purposes.

ISLAND QUARRY

Composed *c.* July 1927–*c.* latter part of 1927; first published December 1927. Sheet 11 of the folder provides the present text, except for the title in sheet 11, "Quarry", which is emended by the title in the contents page of the folder and by the title used in *transition*, 9 (December 1927), p. 132.

OLD SONG

Composed *c.* mid–1927 or earlier; first published August 1927. The twelfth sheet of the folder, which is the only extant version of the poem as prepared by HC, is the source of the present text. The conventional form of the poem, and its title in particular, suggest that HC had composed "Old Song" during a much earlier period in his development.

THE IDIOT

Composed and revised *c.* August 1926–*c.* 1928; first published December 1927. The latest version is sheet 13 in the folder, which provides this edition's text. Line 14: "*A*" emends "*Á*"; it was also corrected in *transition*, 9 (December 1927), p. 135.

A NAME FOR ALL

Composed *c.* October–November 1928; first published April 1929. Sheet 15 of the folder provides the present text. No other version prepared by HC has survived.

BACARDI SPREADS THE EAGLE'S WING

Composed and revised *c.* latter part of 1927 and then between *c.* February 1930 and March 1932; first published December 1927. The present text is based on the *Contempo* printing of HC's 11 March 1932 enclosure of the poem to that periodical, which published it 5 July 1932, page 1. This is HC's last version of the poem. There is no evidence to suggest that the *Contempo* title "WING" (instead of "WINGS", which appears in none of HC's extant documents of the poem) was not the poet's intended form.

IMPERATOR VICTUS

Composed *c.* 1927. The folder's sheet 17, which has HC's autograph emendations in pencil, is the only extant version of the poem as prepared by HC and thus provides the present edition's text.

ROYAL PALM

Composed *c.* July 1927–*c.* late 1927; first published December 1927. The present text uses sheet 18 of the folder as its source since it is HC's latest extant version of the poem. Line 7: "elephantine" emends "elaphantine".

HC correctly spelled the word in his 18 July 1927 copy of the poem sent to Yvor Winters.

THE AIR PLANT

Composed *c*. July–October 1927; first published February 1928. The present edition is based on HC's last version of the poem, the folder's sheet 21. Line 10: "stricken" emends "striken". The former appears in five of HC's documents of the poem, including his "corrected version" sent to Yvor Winters.

THE HURRICANE

Composed and revised between *c*. summer 1927 and *c*. February–July 1931; first published December 1927. The text of the present edition is based on sheet 23 of the folder. It is the last version among several prepared by HC.

KEY WEST Folder Subsection

KEY WEST

Composed *c*. 1927. The present edition's text is based on HC's latest typescript with autograph emendations, sheet 24 of the folder. Sheets 25 and 26 are earlier drafts. It is moot as to whether HC left line 13 in finished form or not. Sheet 24 clearly is not a fair copy that HC prepared as his final version of "Key West."

—AND BEES OF PARADISE

Composed July 1927. The present text is from sheet 27 of the folder, dated "7/28/27," which is HC's only extant document of the poem.

TO EMILY DICKINSON

Composed November 1926–*c*. June 1927; first published June 1927. The folder's sheet 28 provides the present edition's text. It is HC's last version of the poem among several other earlier ones.

MOMENT FUGUE

Composed *c.* 1929; first published February 1929. The present text is based on sheet 29 of HC's folder. It is HC's only extant original document of the poem.

BY NILUS ONCE I KNEW . . .

Composed *c.* 1927. Sheet 30 of the folder, which is HC's only surviving original document of the poem, provides the present edition's text.

TO SHAKESPEARE

Composed *c.* November 1926–mid-1930. The text is based on sheet 31 of the folder. It is HC's latest extant version of the poem.

Poems Uncollected But Published by Crane

The text of each of the following poems, presented in the chronological order of its publication by HC in uncollected form, is based on the published form that it took during the poet's life, unless the printer's copy or some other reliable, authoritative text is extant. If a poem appeared in more than one printed version in HC's lifetime but exists in no document that he inscribed or typed, this edition's text is chosen for the particular reasons discussed below.

C33

Composed *c.* first half of 1916; published in *Bruno's Weekly*, 3 (23 September 1916), p. 1008. Line 6: "thruths" emended to "truths". Line 12: "through" emended from "thru" since no evidence suggests that HC intended the latter as his final version. Though it may have been HC's and/or the *Bruno's Weekly* form, the standard spelling is justified on aesthetic grounds in the context of "C 33."

OCTOBER–NOVEMBER

Composed *c.* 1916; first published in *The Pagan*, 1 (November–December 1916), p. 33. Line 2: "mists;" instead of "mists,—" (*The Pagan Anthology* [ed. Joseph Kling] (New York: Pagan Publishing Company, [1918]), p. 18), since the 1916 version would have been set up from HC's printer's copy or a version of it prepared by or for Joseph Kling, though it is possible that HC rather than Kling altered line 2 in the *Anthology*.

THE HIVE

Composed *c*. February 1917; published in *The Pagan*, 1 (March 1917), p. 36.

FEAR

Composed *c*. early 1917; first published in *The Pagan*, 1–2 (April–May 1917), p. 11. The present text is based on *The Pagan Anthology* (New York: Pagan Publishing Company, [1918], p. 18) because the line 7 "me . . ." is more accurate than "me. . . ." in the 1917 printing.

ANNUNCIATIONS

Composed *c*. early 1917; published in *The Pagan*, 1–2 (April–May 1917), p. 11.

ECHOES

Composed *c*. 1917; published in *The Pagan*, 2 (October–November 1917), p. 39. The text of the present edition is based on a black carbon typescript dated 13 November 1918, which was transcribed by a Liveright staff secretary from HC's enclosure of a group of poems to Charles C. Bubb, who operated The Church Head Press. The transcript of HC's enclosure to Bubb is a revision of the *Pagan* version. The carbon copy is closer to HC's final intentions in the absence of the original document from which it was transcribed. Line 1: "Slivers" emends "Slivvers" in the two sources of the text.

THE BATHERS

Composed *c*. 1917; published in *The Pagan*, 2 (December 1917), p. 19. Line 9: "wrong . . . ." emends "wrong . . . . .".

MODERN CRAFT

Composed *c*. 1917; published in *The Pagan*, 2 (January 1918), p. 37. Line 5: "lillies" in *The Pagan* may have been HC's and/or a compositorial error, but is emended to "lilies" in the present text.

CARMEN DE BOHEME

Composed *c*. 1916; published in *Bruno's Bohemia*, 1 (18 March 1918), p. 2. The following are emended since there is no evidence that HC intended the solecisms: line 9: "cresendo's" to "crescendo's"; line 12: "—and" for "————and"; and line 20: ' "Carmen!" ' for ' "Carmen!",'.

EXILE

Composed *c*. early 1918; published as "Carrier Letter" in *The Pagan*, 2–3 (April–May 1918), p. 20. The basis for the text is the transcript of HC's 13 November 1918 revised form of this poem. See the note for "Echoes."

POSTSCRIPT

Composed *c*. early- to mid-1918; published in *The Pagan*, 2–3 (April–May 1918), p. 20. HC's ring-binder notebook page 89 provides the text for this edition because it is certain that he prepared it. Though the *Pagan* version may be an exact printing of the copy that HC submitted to that little magazine, of which he was then one of the associate editors, the notebook version that HC typed and placed in his three-ring binder has more authority in the absence of conclusive evidence that the *Pagan* variants were made by HC.

FORGETFULNESS

Composed *c*. summer 1918; first published in *The Pagan*, 3 (August–September 1918), p. 15. The present text is from the above, which accords with page 91's text in HC's three-ring notebook. The poem was also printed in *A Second Pagan Anthology* (New York: Pagan Publishing Company, [1919]), p. 17, but its variant "motionless" instead of "motionless," in line 4 has no basis in HC's extant documents.

TO PORTAPOVITCH

Composed *c*. latter part of 1917–*c*. early 1919. Published in *The Modern School*, 6 (March 1919), p. 80. The basis for the present text is page 63 of the ring-binder notebook, which contains HC's final version of the poem.

LEGENDE

Composed *c*. late 1918–*c*. late 1919. Published in *The Modernist*, 3 (November 1919), p. 28. Page 59 of HC's three-ring notebook contains the text on which the present edition is based because that text is the latest surviving form of the poem that HC prepared. Line 7: "the sea" in *The Modernist* instead of "sea" has no basis in HC's extant documents of the poem.

INTERIOR

Composed *c*. late 1918–*c*. late 1919. Published in *The Modernist*, 3 (November 1919), p. 28. The text is from page 57 of the ring-binder notebook. In it HC's final revisions were made when the poem was already in press, so that he could no longer revise for *The Modernist*, nor when the poem had just appeared in print.

PORPHYRO IN AKRON

Composed June 1920–latter part of 1921. Published in *The Double Dealer*, 2 (August–September 1921), p. 53. Pages 71, 73, and 75 of HC's binder notebook provide the text for the present edition, since they were prepared by the poet just before or after the poem appeared in *The Double Dealer*, some of whose variants appear in some of HC's extant original documents of the poem. Line 4, "stubbornness" in *The Double Dealer* corrects "stubborness" in HC's notebook. Line 45: "pays . . . ?" in *The Double Dealer* emends "pays. . ?". Line 52: the seven dots evoke a sense of wistfulness.

A PERSUASION

Composed May 1921. Published in *The Measure*, 8 (October, 1921), p. 14. HC's page 87 in the notebook version of the poem provides the text for this edition, though it varies from the *Measure*'s version only in its capitalization of all the letters of the title.

THREE LOCUTIONS DES PIERROTS

Composed *c.* May 1922; published in *The Double Dealer*, 3 (May 1922), pp. 261–262. The present text is based on pages 77–[78] in HC's ring notebook, the only extant authoritative document of the poem, since the title in *The Double Dealer* and its line 11 in III with "now" instead of "now," have no basis in the one surviving text prepared by the poet. No conclusive evidence suggests that HC intended the title "THREE LOCUTIONS DES PIERROTS," instead of just "Locutions Des Pierrots" (in *The Double Dealer*), ultimately to appear otherwise than in his notebook's form.

THE GREAT WESTERN PLAINS

Composed *c.* summer–fall of 1922. Published in *Gargoyle*, 3 (August 1927), p. [7]. Page 81 of HC's notebook provides the present text because the conventionally capitalized first letter of every line in *Gargoyle* has no basis in HC's one surviving document of the poem.

AMERICA'S PLUTONIC ECSTASIES

Composed January 1923; published in *S4N*, 4 (May–August 1923), pp. [56–57]. HC's page 55 in his binder notebook is taken as the basis for the present edition's text because it is the latest extant form prepared by the poet. The following variants in *S4N* appear in none of HC's surviving documents of the poem: line 15, "righteousness and yet" instead of his notebook's "righteousness. Yet"; line 19, "all." instead of "all"; and line 23, "FREEEE-er" instead of "FREE-ER". Line 1: "preferring" corrects "prefering"; and line 10: "unbelievably" in a 1923 original source and in *S4N* emends "unbelieveably" in the notebook version.

INTERLUDIUM

Composed *c.* November–December 1923–*c.* mid-1924; published in *1924*, 1 (July 1924), p. 2. The notebook form of "Interludium" provides the present text because it is the latest extant version after two earlier ones prepared by HC. The following variants in *1924* comprise those that do not appear in HC's extant documents of the poem: "Montagne," instead of "Montagne" in the notebook's dedication; line 7: "unresigned—" instead of "unresigned"; line 8 omitted; line 11: "untried:" instead of "untried,

—"; line 12: "now," instead of "now"; and line 13: "thee" instead of "thee—".

MARCH

Composed *c.* early 1927; published in *larus: The Celestial Visitor*, 1 (March 1927), p. 14.

THE BROKEN TOWER

Composed February–March 1932; published in *The New Republic*, 71 (8 June 1932), p. 91. The basis for the present edition's text is HC's type-written and autograph manuscript enclosed in a letter postmarked 29 March 1932. It is HC's latest extant version of "The Broken Tower" among several other earlier ones. The following in *The New Republic* appear in none of HC's extant documents of the poem: line 6, "town" for "tower"; line 24, "hope" for "hope,"; and line 35, "pebbles" for "pebbles,".

Poems Unpublished by Crane

The verse that HC left in unpublished, incomplete, or merely fragmentary form is arranged in as accurate a chronological order by date of composition as evidence permits. Verse attributed to HC—five in all—variant texts, or works excluded from a longer sequence of poems, such as "Lenses," which HC deleted from *The Bridge*, have been omitted from this reader's edition but will appear in an already prepared variant textual edition of the poems of HC.

A SONG FOR HAPPY FEAST DAYS

Composed December 1914. This quatrain is dated and inscribed by HC below the last line of "To Aunt Alice | from | Harold Crane | Xmas of 1914." The earliest extant verse by HC, it appears on a blank preliminary leaf of *The Complete Poetical Works of Robert Burns* (New York: Crowell, n.d.). Aunt Alice was HC's father's sister.

SONNET ("Ere elfish Night . . .")

Composed *c.* 1915–1916. The text in the present edition is based on a typescript among HC's papers. HC's autograph draft of this "Sonnet" has also survived. Young HC's following solecisms are emended: Lines 5 and 13, "shallt" to "shalt"; line 10, "vallies" to "valleys"; and line 12, "Cecelia" to "Cecilia"; 'gift".' to 'gift." '

THE MOTH THAT GOD MADE BLIND

Composed *c*. late 1915–mid–December 1917. This text is based on HC's one extant original document of the poem. Line 12: "jeweleries" emended to "jewelleries"; line 23: "himbly" to "humbly"; line 33: "Til" to "Till"; and line 38: "octupus" to "octopus".

TO EARTH

Composed *c*. late 1916–1918. The present text is provided by the transcript of HC's 13 November 1918 enclosure of the poem in a letter. See the note for "Echoes."

MEDUSA

Composed *c*. late 1916–1918. The text derives from the same source as "To Earth" above.

MEDITATION

Composed *c*. late 1916–1918. This text is based on the same source as the two above. Line 18: "shalt" emends "shallt".

EPISODE OF HANDS

Composed April 1920. HC's one's surviving typescript of the poem enclosed in a letter is the basis for the present edition's text. Line 11: "fingers wound" emends "fingers fingers wound".

THE BRIDGE OF ESTADOR

Composed *c*. November 1920–April 1921. HC's 10 April 1921 enclosure of the poem in a letter is the last version among several others and thus provides the present text. Line 26: "Seen" emends "See"; the "n" is added to correct the inadvertent omission. Crane's error derived from an incomplete alteration of the phrase "may . . . See" to "have . . . Seen". Line 29: "arches | To" corrects HC's typographical error of "arches to | To".

AFTER JONAH

Composed *c.* 1922–1926. The present text is based on HC's one extant typescript of "After Jonah."

EUCLID AVENUE

Composed *c.* January–February 1923. The present edition's text is provided by HC's last version of the poem after four earlier drafts.

OF AN EVENING . . .

Composed November–December 1923. HC's one surviving document of this parody of E. E. Cummings is the basis for the present text.

WHAT NOTS ?

Composed December 1923. The present edition's text is provided by HC's one extant typescript of "What Nots ?" enclosed in a late December letter. Line 10: "Laocoön" emends "Laocöon".

IN A COURT

Composed *c.* March 1924. The text of this edition is based on the only surviving version of this poem that HC had originally sent to *The Dial*, which rejected it; namely, *Literary America*, 1 (September 1934), p. 14.

WITH A PHOTOGRAPH . . .

Composed October 1924. The present text is provided by HC's one extant typescript of this occasional piece intended for HC's aunt and godmother, who was going on a cruise—but not to Spain. Line 5: "Manhattan" emends "Manhatten"; line 13: "into" corrects "iinto".

SUPPLICATION TO THE MUSES . . .

Composed *c.* 1926–1927. HC's one surviving typescript with autograph emendations is the basis for the present edition's text, including HC's hyphenations, and his lineation to avoid line-reference problems. Line 2 of epigraph: "seagull's" emends "seagulls"; line 8: "it!" for "it!' "; line 11: "harangued" for "haranged"; line 20: "night" for "nightt"; line 23, "till" for "til" and "equivocating" for "eqivocating"; line 26: 'eternity!" ' for 'eternity!", '; line 28: "derelict" for "derilict"; line 30: "dermatologists" for "dermetoligists" or "dermotolagists"; and line 32: "fratricide. . . ." for "fratercide . . ."

ETERNITY

Composed *c.* November 1926–September 1927. The only extant typescript with HC's hand in ink provides the present text. The terminal punctuation of both epigraph lines is emended to italic, since it is part of the adage and not HC's. Line 28: no stanza break.

THE SAD INDIAN

Composed *c.* latter half of 1926–1930. HC's one surviving holograph of "The Sad Indian" is the basis for the present edition's text.

HIEROGLYPHIC

Composed *c.* March 1932. The later version of this text, which HC typed after his earlier red-pencil draft, provides the present form of this epigram.

Incomplete Works

THIS WAY WHERE NOVEMBER . . .

Composed November 1923. The present text is provided by HC's one extant typewritten and autograph manuscript. Between stanzas 3 and 4, "(other verses even less developed—poem | ends with following lines" is typewritten by HC. This edition presents lines 19–21 as the last stanza in this incomplete work.

THOU CANST READ NOTHING . . .

Composed *c.* 1924–1926. HC's one surviving typescript of this work is the basis for the present edition's text.

TO LIBERTY

Composed *c.* 1924–1927. The single extant typescript with HC's hand in pencil provides the text for this edition.

TO THE EMPRESS JOSEPHINE'S STATUE

Composed *c.* 1926–1927. HC's second extant holograph is the basis for the present text. The emendations in this edition's text are made only to correct spelling or to alter punctuation for coherent syntax in HC's ambiguous, incomplete work. Line 1: "contain" replaces "contain,"; line 2: "caressed" for "carressed"; line 5: "Caribbean" for "Caribeanean"; line 6: the first "who" replaces "Who"; line 7: "rushes," instead of "rushes" and "charge," replaces "charge"; line 8: "our" for "are", "hoodwink" for "hood-wink", and "sputum," instead of "sputum"; line 12: "Caribbean" for "Caribean"; line 14: "memory—" instead of "memory"; and line 15: "care." replaces "care".

A POSTSCRIPT

Composed *c.* 1926–1928. The text of the present edition is based on HC's one surviving typescript of this work, which contains his ink alterations. Line 7: "Remember" replaces "Remembers" and "lilies" emends "lilies," HC apparently having neglected to delete the comma when revising; line 11: "porters," instead of "porters"; and line 16: "Antillean" corrects "Antillian".

THE PILLAR AND THE POST

Composed *c.* 1926–1929. HC's single extant holograph of this work is the basis for the present edition's text.

THE VISIBLE THE UNTRUE

Composed *c.* 1927–1929. The second draft made by HC for this work provides the present text. Line 2: "terrible" emends "terribel"; line 5:

"fingernails" for "finger nails"; line 11: "Zeppelin" instead of "Zepplin"; line 13: "confidence" for "confidacne"; line 14: "toothaches" replaces "tooth aches"; and line 18: "me . . ." emends "me—, ..." which has a five-hyphen dash.

A TRAVELLER BORN

Composed *c.* first half of July 1930–*c.* April 1931. The present text is based on HC's typed and autograph latest draft for lines 1–12 of this work, and on an earlier draft for lines 13–28, since none of the several original sources for "A Traveller Born" has a text with all the lines of the work. Line 2: "abbé" replaces "abbie"; line 3: "Pernod" emends "Pernot"; line 4: "Its" emends ", its"; line 10: "crucifix" for "cricifix"; line 11: "Pasteur" for "Pasture"; line 16: "silhouette" for "sillouhette"; line 17: "the midnight" corrects "the my midnight"; line 21: "Less" emends "less"; line 23: "pilot" for "pilote"; and line 25: "sincere" replaces "sincere,".

HAVANA ROSE

Composed *c.* early May 1931. The one extant holograph prepared by HC provides the present edition's text. HC clearly accommodated the line-breaks of his poem in prose to the space available on the two sheets of his text of "Havana Rose." However, this edition accords with HC's lineation to avoid confusion in line references.

Line 1: HC inscribed "horse" clearly above deleted "house". It is used metaphorically in conjunction with "spurred" and "horsemanship" in lines 17, 21. HC revised the literal reference from his "house" to the figurative implication of spurring his Pegasus "for action . . . in Mexico." Regarding a literal, autobiographical interpretation for HC's clearly inscribed, figurative "horse" see John Unterecker, *Notes to the First Edition of Voyager A Life of Hart Crane* (New York: Farrar, Straus and Giroux, 1970), p. 665 n.

Line 4: "fond" replaces "fond,"; line 5: "cheroot" emends "cherut"; line 6: "pistol—" for "pistol"; line 7: "mid-wind" for "mid wind" and "milk-light" for "milk light"; line 9: "lofty," emends "lofty"; line 10: "Doctor's" for "doctors"; lines 13, 17, 27: "Doctor" instead of "doctor"; line 15: "flashed . . ." for "flashed. . . ." and "whirled . . ." for "whirled. . . ."; line 21: "horsemanship," instead of "horsemanship—"; and line 33: 'birth." ' replaces 'birth.'

PURGATORIO

Composed *c.* 1931–1932. The present text is based on HC's only surviving holograph of "Purgatorio." The last two lines of the present edition are given in the incomplete state in which HC left them. Line 3: "sputum" emends "spootum"; line 9: "too-keen . . . too-soft" emends "too keen . . . too soft"; line 10: "grow?" for "grow."; line 16: "town?" for "town"; and line 17: "anew," replaces "anew".

THE CIRCUMSTANCE

Composed *c.* 10–21 September 1931–*c.* March–April 1932. HC's latest version, after two earlier ones, of "The Circumstance" provides the present text. Line 1: "anointed" emends "annointed" and "coruscated" replaces "corruscated"; line 12: "and" corrects "And"; line 17: "Stone . . ." emends "Stone. . . ."; line 21: "lightning" for "lightening"; and line 22: "winds of time)" replaces "winds) [*deleted dash*] of time". HC's alteration of line 22 is incomplete. He did not delete the parenthesis at "winds)" and add the closing parenthesis after "time)" for coherent syntax.

Fragments

TO BUDDHA

Composed *c.* March 1923–fall 1924. The present edition's text is based on HC's one extant document, a pencil holograph. The title is emended from "Bhudda" to "BUDDHA."

WHERE GABLES PACK . . .

Composed 13 April 1923. HC's inclusion of this fragment into his letter to Charlotte Rychtarik is the source of the present text.

WELL/WELL/NOT-AT-ALL

Composed *c.* 23 April 1923. The present edition's text is based on HC's typewritten postcard to Charlotte Rychtarik. Line 4: "Ruf wie" emends "ruhf vie".

YOU ARE THAT FRAIL . . .

Composed *c.* 1924–1926. HC's one extant typescript of this fragment provides the present edition's text.

THE MASTERS

Composed *c.* 1924–1927. The text is based on HC's one surviving typescript of "The Masters." Line 2: "hereafter." emended from "hereafter" for syntactic coherence. Line 4: "overrule" replaces "overule". The asterisks in line 5 are HC's, as is the absence of terminal punctuation in this fragment.

HER EYES HAD . . .

Composed *c.* May 1925. HC's one extant holograph of this fragment is the basis for the present edition's text. The lower-case first letters of lines 3, 6, 9, and 10 have been altered to capitals in this edition. Line 5: "privilege" replaces "priviledge".

O MOON, THOU COOL . . .

Composed *c.* latter part of 1925–1929. The text herein is based on HC's typescript with his autograph emendations. HC left line 4 in particular in fragmentary form. There are two lines of text below an extra spacing and a horizontal line drawn across HC's sheet of paper. The two lines are omitted from the present edition, since they are also indented far left of lines 1–11, all of which suggests that HC had not yet intended the omitted passage to be part of the rest of the fragment. Line 10: "buckwheat" replaces "buckwehat".

THE SEA RAISED UP . . .

Composed *c.* winter of 1926–1927. The second extant draft of this fragment, as typewritten by HC, is the basis for the present text.

SO DREAM THY SAILS . . .

Composed *c.* 1926–1928. HC's one surviving typescript with his pencil emendations provides this edition's text. Brom Weber has stated that "men" in line 2 is "HC's slip of the pen" (see *The Complete Poems and Selected Letters and Prose of Hart Crane* [New York: Liveright, 1966], p. 289). However, no evidence in the fragment's original source suggests that it is; rather, HC meticulously corrected errors in his typescript, though the poet did type "fragment note" in the top left and allowed the text to remain unfinished. The evidence suggests that HC intended line 2 to read "men" as the indirect object of "speak". "That I may speak *for* thy drownèd men again" is HC's meaning, given the archaic diction of the stanza. Line 2: "drownèd" replaces "drownéd"; and line 12: "Imprisoned" emends "imprisoned", and the word "and" is used instead of "&".

I HAVE THAT SURE ENCLITIC . . .

Composed *c.* 1926–1929. The present text is based on HC's only extant document of this fragment, namely an ink holograph. Line 2: "fact." emended from "fact" for syntactic coherence; line 4: "forebear's" replaces "forbear's"; and line 5: "Gorillas" instead of "Gorilla's".

SHALL I SUBSUME . . .

Composed *c.* 1927–1929. HC's single extant typescript of this fragment is the basis for this edition's text. Line 5: "circumvention" emends "circumventation"; line 8: "reflection" instead of "refecltion"; line 10: "jealousy" corrects "jealosy"; line 11: "cameos," corrects "cameos,,"; line 12: "explore" for "axplore"; and line 13: "is" replaces "i".

TENDERNESS AND RESOLUTION

Composed *c.* 1927–1929. The present text is based on HC's one extant holograph of this fragment. The title is taken from HC's first line. Line 2: "sudden pillow" emends "sudden—pillow": line 5: "Sagittarius" instead of "Sagitarrius"; line 8: "variants—" emends "variants"; and line 9: "Charms" for "Charmes".

TIME CANNOT BE WORN . . .

Composed *c.* 1927—1929. HC's typewritten and autograph manuscript that follows his earlier draft is the source of this edition's text.

I ROB MY BREAST . . .

Composed *c*. 26 March 1929. The present text is provided by HC's one extant holograph of this fragment. The lowercase first letters of lines 14–17 are altered to capitals. Line 5: "dilemma" for "dillema"; line 6: "Across" for "Accross"; line 7: "stricken" for "striken"; and line 14: ' "wreckage" ' emends ' "wreckage'.

ENRICH MY RESIGNATION . . .

Composed *c*. fall 1929. The one surviving typescript of this fragment with HC's hand in ink and pencil is the source of the present edition's text. Line 1: "those far" corrects "those those far"; line 5: "Extinction" emends "extinction"; line 7: "Dionysius" for "Dyonisius"; and line 10: "unlaced" emends "unclaced"; "thou" replaces "thous". Lines 7–11 are canceled in pencil (but lines 1–6 HC revised in ink); the tentative deletion is retained as part of this fragment, given its coherence with lines 1–6.

ALL THIS . . .

Composed *c*. late 1929. HC's one extant holograph of this fragment provides the present edition's text. Line 10: "Translated" for "translated"; line 11: "across" for "accross"; line 12: "lullabies" emends "lullabyes"; and line 15: "fifth" instead of "fith".

THE ALERT PILLOW . . .

Composed *c*. latter part of July–*c*. early August 1930. HC's one extant holograph of this fragment provides the text herein. Line 1: "hayseed" emends "hay-seeds"; line 7: "Scythes" replaces "Schythes".

THERE ARE THE LOCAL . . .

Composed *c*. August 1930. The one surviving holograph in HC's hand in pencil is the source of the present text. Line 2: "boughs—" emends "boughs" for clarity. Line 4: "Like" emends "The ['drift of *deleted*] like [*added above*]".

DUST NOW IS . . .

Composed *c.* August 1930. HC's single extant typescript with pencil emendations is the basis for this edition's text of the fragment.

THEY WERE THERE . . .

Composed *c.* April 1931–April 1932. The text of the present edition is based on HC's one surviving typewritten and autograph manuscript of this fragment. Line 6: "dispel" instead of "dispell"; line 7: "constructs" for "contructs"; line 10: "their" for "thier"; line 11: "lorgnette" for "lorngnette"; and line 16: "tourists" for "toursists".

TO CONQUER VARIETY

Composed *c.* April 1931–April 1932. The single extant HC holograph of this fragment is the source of the text in this edition. The final five dots are all given as HC inscribed them, contrary to this edition's convention for ellipses. This has been done to allow the fragmentary nature of the piece to remain as HC left it. Line 6: "dispossessed" emends "dispossosessed".

Index of First Lines

Index of Titles